The Bible Tells Me So

THIS IS THE ENEMY

Both read the Bible day and night,
But thou read'st black where I read white.

—William Blake (1757–1827),
The Everlasting Gospel (c. 1818).

Jesus loves me—this I know,
For the Bible tells me so.

—Anna Bartlett Warner (1827–1915),
The Love of Jesus (1858)

The Bible Tells Me So

Uses and Abuses of
Holy Scripture

Jim Hill and Rand Cheadle

Anchor Books/Doubleday New York London Toronto Sydney Auckland

AN ANCHOR BOOK

PUBLISHED BY DOUBLEDAY

a division of Bantam Doubleday Dell Publishing Group, Inc.

1540 Broadway, New York, New York 10036

ANCHOR BOOKS, DOUBLEDAY, and the portrayal of an anchor
are trademarks of Doubleday, a division of
Bantam Doubleday Dell Publishing Group, Inc.

Book Design by Gretchen Achilles

Library of Congress Cataloging-in-Publication Data

Hill, Jim, 1959–
The Bible tells me so : uses and abuses of Holy Scripture /
Jim Hill and Rand Cheadle. — 1st ed.
p.   cm.
Includes bibliographical references (p.   ).
1. Bible—Use—United States.   2. Bible—Influences—United States.
3. Christianity and politics.   4. Christianity and culture.
I. Cheadle, Rand.   II. Title.
BS538.7.H55   1996
220.6—dc20   94-41097
                                                              CIP

ISBN 0-385-47695-7

Contents

Part Six:
Science, Medicine, and the World

Jesus wept.
—John 11:35

A Brief Guide to the Use and Abuse of Scriptures

"Search the scriptures . . ."

—John 5:39

"*Scrutamini scripturas* [Let us look at the scriptures]. These two words have undone the world."

—John Selden (1584–1654)

A reading of the Bible can offer strength, wisdom, inspiration, and hope in the face of hopelessness.

The Bible has also been used to maintain political power and wealth, wage wars, control populations, and regulate behavior. It has provided reason for persecuting minorities and enemies. And it has been pressed into service to confront persecution, to empower the weak and outcast, and to fight for justice.

This little book is not about the message of the Bible. Rather, it's a brief survey showing how the Bible has been selectively used as a tool. And how, with Bible in hand, religious and political leaders have felt justified in promoting policies that will affect the lives of others. This is not an attack on religion, the Bible, or the Church. Our purpose is simply to call attention to intolerance, injustice, and blind, unquestioning allegiance to people and institutions that seek to hurt and oppress others, with the simple justification "It's in the Bible."

We also tried to acknowledge a few of the many positive aspects of the Bible's influence, and how traditionally oppressed groups have found their own redemption in the same pages.

Scholars, historians, and theologians have gone into fascinating detail on the impact of biblical interpretation on society. Many others have emphasized their own viewpoints or biblical interpretations, carrying on a personal debate with the Bible or the church. We encourage you to read and study their work.

Our goal was to provide, in a quick, accessible way, an awareness of the wide range of issues for which the Bible has been used. The brief essays, along with the accompanying prints, photographs, and illustrations, are intended to convey the spirit of the times and an overview of the subjects in question. Most important, we've highlighted a few examples of the verses that have been selectively used to interpret these subjects.

To some, this may seem to be an oversimplified approach.

But for most of those who use the Bible to justify or condemn, whether out of serious conviction or for mere convenience, it's a simple procedure. Selected verses make everything crystal clear. The proof's right there, they say, in the Bible.

As you read, you might want to look for some general patterns: how the Scriptures have been used to defy or corroborate the law, the political system, medicine, or science; how their interpretation can be used to protect or challenge the powerful or to hinder or instigate change; and how people use the Bible to define themselves or another group.

You may embrace some chapters and find others offensive, humorous, blasphemous, or preposterous. Or you may simply dismiss some issues presented as the product of another place and time. Our reaction was the same.

But just imagine yourself in some other place and time, where you could have been the target of a biblically based attack. Or where the Bible was used as a valuable tool in proving individual worth, following conscience, or shaping public agenda.

After you've finished reading *The Bible Tells Me So,* you'll probably become more aware of references to the Bible in public debate. You may decide that church and state aren't quite as "separate" as many claim. And you'll undoubtedly begin to notice how often many passages are completely ignored.

Whether you begin to question the motivations of Bible-quoting politicians, opinion shapers, and authorities is up to you.

The authors would appreciate your thoughts and opinions. Write to us at:

The Bible Tells Me So
c/o Anchor Books
1540 Broadway
New York, NY 10036

Or online:

America Online: BibleTells
Internet: BibleTells@aol.com

Authors' Notes

Verses shown in *The Bible Tells Me So* are from the King James Version of the Bible, which is still the most commonly used translation.

For each issue, our objective was to find the most pertinent, most frequently used scriptural line of reasoning and then show how such reasoning has been reflected in the words and actions of influential leaders or the public at large.

The examples collected here are the result of exhaustive research, and have also been retrieved from a lifetime of personal experiences, from sermons, Sunday school classes, rallies and protests, the news media, college lectures, religious tracts, and countless books. Television, talk radio, and televangelists continue to be an excellent resource. Many readers will recall still more verses used to address other issues.

The subjects discussed here are intentionally the most general and far-reaching. The notes will help in further exploration of specific issues. While this book includes some of the primary verses relating to a particular topic, note that there are countless other verses that can and have been put into use.

Acknowledgments

We are grateful to many people who both encouraged and helped us in the final realization of this project.

Mr. and Mrs. Robert Kensinger kindly allowed us to use many prints and engravings from their personal collection. Among the many helpful professionals at the Library of Congress, we would like to thank Maja Keech and Jane Van Nimmen, reference specialists in the prints and photographs division. Special thanks to Charles Sens, music specialist at the Library of Congress, who provided invaluable guidance and direction.

We would also like to thank the many organizations and institutions who have permitted us to use images from their collections.

As guides through the publishing labyrinth, special thanks goes to Tom Dupree of Bantam Books for his enthusiasm, encouragement, and comments in the early phases of the book; Charles Conrad, our editor at Anchor; and literary agent Gordon Kato. We are most grateful for the support of family and friends, especially Holly Williams, who helped to get the ball rolling.

Part One

People and Their Place in Society

Behold, how good and how pleasant it is for brethren to dwell together in unity!

—Psalm 133:1

To Justify Slavery

There is no specific condemnation of slavery in the Bible. The Old Testament presents guidelines for slaveholders, including advice in taking care of human property. The New Testament describes the relationship between master and slave.

Poor British subjects often became indentured servants, serving their "own kind" for seven years (echoing the book of Exodus); African blacks' servitude usually ended only at death. The first ship bearing slaves bound for America landed in Jamestown, Virginia, in 1619, beginning what would become known as "the peculiar institution."

In the late eighteenth century, the Reverend William Graham, rector and principal instructor of Liberty Hall Academy (now Washington and Lee University in Lexington, Virginia), annually lectured the senior class, using the Bible as a critical defense of slavery. Graham believed that Christianity was not a tool to change public policies, but

Detail of illustration by Thomas Nast (1864)

to bring the message of salvation to everyone, regardless of his or her place in life—"husband or wife, parent or child, master or servant."

Religious leaders used the Bible to teach slaves not to challenge or strike their masters, and to willingly accept punishment (I Peter 2:21). It was common, though not always strictly enforced, to forbid slaves to learn how to read. Of course, this kept the Bible unavailable to them except as it was shared by their masters or, eventually, by some literate slave or free black preacher. In

"Liberty, then, when forced on a people unfit for it, would, instead of a blessing, be a curse . . . [man's] natural state is . . . the one for which his Creator made him . . ."

—South Carolina Senator John C. Calhoun (1782–1850), from his "Speech on the Importance of Domestic Slavery"

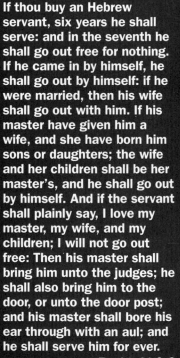

If thou buy an Hebrew servant, six years he shall serve: and in the seventh he shall go out free for nothing. If he came in by himself, he shall go out by himself: if he were married, then his wife shall go out with him. If his master have given him a wife, and she have born him sons or daughters; the wife and her children shall be her master's, and he shall go out by himself. And if the servant shall plainly say, I love my master, my wife, and my children; I will not go out free: Then his master shall bring him unto the judges; he shall also bring him to the door, or unto the door post; and his master shall bore his ear through with an aul; and he shall serve him for ever.

—Exodus 21:2–6

4

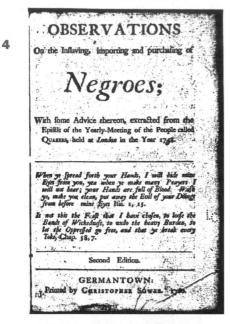

A Quaker document of 1760 quotes the Bible to make a point regarding the evils of slavery.

"Slaves were forbidden to lift a hand against a Christian, even in self defense . . . Anyone could be a slave, whether converted to Christianity or not, provided they were not of Christian parentage or country."

—Historian W. O. Blake in 1857 discussing the 1682 Slave Code of Virginia

"There shall never be any bond slavery, villenage, nor captivity among us, unless it be lawful captives, taken in just wars, and such strangers as willingly sell themselves or are sold unto us, and these shall have all the liberties and Christian usages which the law of God established in Israel requires . . ."

—Massachusetts Slave Code, 1641, based on Mosaic Law, one of the first Scriptural justifications of the institution

many places, religious meetings were forbidden without white witnesses.

Christianity became a way to add value to slaves. According to Kenneth Stampp in *The Peculiar Institution:* "when southern clergymen became ardent defenders of slavery, the master class could look upon organized religion as an ally . . . the gospel, instead of becoming a means of creating trouble and strife, was really the best instrument to preserve peace and good conduct among the negroes." An Alabama judge believed that religious instruction "not only benefits the slave in his moral relations, but enhances his value as an honest, faithful servant and laborer."

While a lot of Christian leaders and laypeople in the South would have been pleased for slavery simply to disappear, pressures from the North prompted many others to put the Bible into service on their side of the debate. Pamphlets, tracts, and lectures declared slavery was a proper institution that cre-

ated an extended Christian family, condoned by the Scriptures.

In 1856, the Reverend Thorton Stringfellow, a Baptist minister from Culpeper County, Virginia, made a succinct summation: ". . . Jesus Christ recognized this institution as one that was lawful among men, and regulated its relative duties . . . I affirm then, first, (and no man denies,) that Jesus Christ has not abolished slavery by a prohibitory command; and second, I affirm, he has introduced no new moral principle which can work its destruction . . ."

During this period, many denominations split. The Southern Baptist Convention, now the largest Protestant organization in the United States, grew out of such a difference of opinion.

In 1844, The Baptist General Convention resolved to allow all its members and congregations to come to their own conclusions about slavery. Shortly thereafter a conflicting statement came from the executive board: "If any

"For all slaveholders with whom I have ever met, religious slaveholders are the worst. I have ever found them the meanest and basest, the most cruel and cowardly, of all others. It was my unhappy lot . . . to belong to a religious slaveholder . . . He always managed to have one or more of his slaves to whip every Monday morning."

—Frederick Douglass,
as quoted from his autobiography (1845)

. . . missionary, having slaves, should insist on retaining them as his property, we could not appoint him. One thing is certain, we can never be a party to an arrangement which would imply [approval] of slavery." Those in the South disagreed. In May 1845, 310 delegates from the Southern churches met in Augusta, Georgia, and organized the separate Southern Baptist Convention.

In 1907, Baptist historian Henry C. Vedder stated that if the Northerners on the executive board "felt as Christian men that obedience to the higher law of God forbade them to carry out their instructions [to ignore the issue of slavery], their honorable course was to resign."

"Flogging the Negro." Scenes of slave mistreatment from *The Suppressed Book About Slavery* (1864).

And if a man smite his servant, or his maid, with a rod, and he die under his hand; he shall be surely punished. Notwithstanding, if he continue a day or two, he shall not be punished: for he is his money.

Exodus 21:20–21

Masters, give unto your servants that which is just and equal; knowing that ye also have a Master in heaven.

—Colossians 4:1

Both thy bondmen, and thy bondmaids, which thou shalt have, shall be of the heathen that are round about you; of them shall ye buy bondmen and bondmaids. Moreover of the children of the strangers that do sojourn among you, of them shall ye buy, and of their families that are with you, which they begat in your land: and they shall be your possession. And ye shall take them as an inheritance for your children after you, to inherit them for a possession; they shall be your bondmen for ever: but over your brethren the children of Israel, ye shall not rule one over another with rigour.

—Leviticus 25:44–46

6

Servants, obey in all things your masters according to the flesh; not with eyeservice, as menpleasers; but in singleness of heart, fearing God.
—Colossians 3:22

Servants, be obedient to them that are your masters according to the flesh, with fear and trembling, in singleness of your heart, as unto Christ.
—Ephesians 6:5

Servants, be subject to your masters with all fear; not only to the good and gentle, but also to the froward. For this is thankworthy, if a man for conscience toward God endure grief, suffering wrongfully. For what glory is it, if, when ye be buffeted for your faults, ye shall take it patiently? but if, when ye do well, and suffer for it, ye take it patiently, this is acceptable with God. For even hereunto were ye called: because Christ also suffered for us, leaving us an example, that ye should follow his steps.
—I Peter 2:18–21

"Joseph Sold Into Slavery." Engraving from a seventeenth-century Bible illustrating Genesis 37.

In June 1995, the Southern Baptist Convention formally apologized for its support of slavery (referring to it as an "original sin") and for its opposition to the civil rights initiatives of the 1950s and 1960s.

". . . Jesus Christ recognized this institution as one that was lawful among men, and regulated its relative duties . . . I affirm then, first, (and no man denies,) that Jesus Christ has not abolished slavery by a prohibitory command . . ."

—Reverend Thorton Stringfellow, a Baptist minister of Culpeper County, Virginia, author of the extensively distributed *A Scriptural View* (1856)

To Justify the Abolishment of Slavery

The concept of slavery was an integral part of nineteenth-century America; those who sought its end, often confronting religious leaders, were considered radicals.

Abolitionists, both blacks and whites inside and outside the Christian mainstream, often concerned themselves with other contemporary issues, such as the banning of alcohol. Their varied goals often canceled each other out: those who could be persuaded to an anti-slavery stance often were unable to support another civil rights cause, such as granting equal rights to women.

Abolitionists found support and

"Where human law 'oerrules Divine,
Beneath the sheriff's hammer fell
My wife and babes,—I call them mine,—
And where they suffer, who can tell?
The hounds are baying on my track,
O Christian! will you send me back?"

—Lyrics to anti-slavery hymn "The Fugitive Slave to the Christian" (1844)

The "Pictorial Illustration of Abolitionism" (1865) concludes with the statement warning that abolitionism "commenced by dividing the Church; it ended by dividing the Union."

justification for their cause in the same Bible used to support slavery. Abolitionist Angelina Grimké referred to her Bible as "my dictionary."

One abolitionist strategy involved "outing" slaveholders among church congregations. William Lloyd Garrison (1805–1879), founder of *The Liberator,* an anti-slavery newspaper, eventually renounced his own church for its pro-slavery stance.

Others took a more direct approach. Nat Turner, a Virginia slave, believing an eclipse to be a sign from God, gathered fifty men and hacked to death fifty-five members of slave-owning families. Horrified Virginians demanded an end to slavery and the deportation of all blacks; the measure missed passage by seven votes.

The Fugitive Slave Law, passed in 1850, called for a fine of one thousand dollars for any person who helped a runaway slave. Clergymen argued against the law, referring to the Old Testament: "Thou shalt not deliver unto his master the servant which is escaped from his master unto

And he that stealeth a man, and selleth him, or if he be found in his hand, he shall surely be put to death.
—Exodus 21:16

And hath made of one blood all nations of men for to dwell on all the face of the earth, and hath determined the times before appointed, and the bounds of their habitation.
—Acts 17:26

And the heart of the Pharaoh was hardened, neither would he let the children of Israel go; as the Lord had spoken by Moses.
—Exodus 9:35

Therefore all things whatsoever ye would that men should do to you, do ye even so to them: for this is the law and the prophets.
—Matthew 7:12

For this, Thou shalt not commit adultery, Thou shalt not kill, Thou shalt not steal, Thou shalt not bear false witness, Thou shalt not covet; and if there be any other commandment, it is briefly comprehended in this saying, namely, Thou shalt love thy neighbour as thyself.
—Romans 13:9

Frontispiece engraving from the abolitionist anthology *The Liberty Bell* (1839)

"When my countrymen shall burn their Bibles, and rescind their famous Declaration of Independence, and reduce themselves to colonial dependence upon the mother country, I will find both time and patience to reason with them on the subject of human rights."
—William Lloyd Garrison, "The Cause of Emancipation" (1839)

thee . . ." (Deuteronomy 23:15). Many runaway slaves aimed for Canada, traveling via The Underground Railroad, a secret network of sympathizers running from the South to the North.

In a critique of minister Josiah Priest's *Bible Defense of Slavery* (1853), a *Baltimore Sun* editorialist blasted back: "Bible defence of slavery! There is no such thing. . . . Slavery is recorded in the Bible and approved, with many degrad-ing characteristics. War is recorded in the Bible, and approved, under what seems to us the extreme of cruelty. But are slavery and war to *endure* for ever because we find them in the Bible? or are they to *cease* at once and for ever because the Bible inculcates peace and brotherhood?"

Many abolitionists, rather than debating the issue, put their biblical interpretations into action through freeing, harboring, and

LITTLE EVA CONVERTING TOPSY.
"In that moment a ray of real belief, a ray of heavenly love, had penetrated the darkness of her heathen soul."

"In that moment a ray of real belief, a ray of heavenly love, had penetrated the darkness of her heathen soul."—nineteenth-century illustration from the influential anti-slavery novel, *Uncle Tom's Cabin, or Life Among the Lowly* (1852), in which Little Eva converts Topsy. Eliza's husband, George, escapes using the Underground Railroad, by which an estimated sixty thousand slaves escaped between 1830 and 1860. Author Harriet Beecher Stowe claimed that the novel was inspired by a vision, thus written by God.

Thou shalt not deliver unto his master the servant which is escaped from his master unto thee: He shall dwell with thee, even among you, in that place which he shall choose in one of thy gates, where it liketh him best: thou shalt not oppress him.
—Deuteronomy 23:15–16

There is neither Jew nor Greek, there is neither bond nor free, there is neither male nor female: for ye are all one in Christ Jesus.
—Galatians 3:28

assisting former slaves. Many Christian abolitionists saw the Civil War as God's punishment for the toleration of slavery by the Southern church.

Many verses defining how people should treat one another, such as the parable of the Good Samaritan (Luke 10:25–37) and the Golden Rule (Matthew 7:12 and Luke 6:31), which were used to promote abolition, have also come in handy in debates over the sanctuary movement, abortion, liberation theology, and civil rights. Many see these as fundamental lessons of the Bible.

Abolitionist woodcut (1837)

AM I NOT A MAN AND A BROTHER?

"The parties in this conflict are not merely Abolitionists and slaveholders—they are atheists, socialists, communists, red republicans, Jacobins on the one side, and the friends of order and regulated freedom on the other. In one word, the world is the battleground—Christianity and atheism the combatants; and the progress of humanity at stake."

—Dr. James H. Tornwell, religious and educational leader of South Carolina (1850)

10

I beseech you therefore, brethren, by the mercies of God, that ye present your bodies a living sacrifice, holy, acceptable unto God, which is your reasonable service. And be not conformed to this world: but be ye transformed by the renewing of your mind, that ye may prove what is that good, and acceptable, and perfect, will of God. For I say, through the grace given unto me, to every man that is among you, not to think of himself more highly than he ought to think; but to think soberly, according as God hath dealt to every man the measure of faith.

—Romans 12:1–3

"Pure-blooded Caucasians—the earth's most endangered species."

—Aryan Nation slogan

White supremacy groups don't usually limit their targets to people of color.

To Justify the Superiority of White Protestants

Most races of people have at one time or another sought ways to prove themselves superior to all others. Strategies relying on religion to accomplish this have traditionally been among the most successful.

Of course, "Caucasians" are not found in the Bible. "Christian Identity" groups use the Bible to prove that the "chosen people," or the "true Israelites," are White American Protestants.

The United States has seen a number of racist "Christian" groups, most notoriously the Ku Klux Klan. While not a denomina-

tion in the strictest sense, the number of Klan members, and their allegiance to their beliefs, could once have easily compared with those of many churches.

The Klan was originally founded in Pulaski, Tennessee, in 1866. But in the 1920s it gained a national following. An estimated more than two million Americans across the country joined the Invisible Empire.

Klansmen openly recruited in churches, attracting members from all levels of society, including the clergy. Rumors of influential members abounded; future president Harry Truman reportedly had taken the vow, as had future Supreme Court Justice Hugo L. Black.

Often, racially oriented groups use the Bible as a symbol, along with the flag, the Cross, and the family. Members often remain allied with mainstream denominations, which frequently have already deemed the group's targets as "inferior/unworthy" or "not saved."

While varying widely, a typical early Klan ceremony, or "Klonvocation," focused on the Bible, set on an altar and opened to Romans 12—"godly conduct, godly nature," a guide to living a Christian life. Included also were an American flag along with an illuminated or "fiery" Cross, sometimes aflame,

The Bible Tells Me So

The FIERY CROSS on HIGH

Copyright 1923 by Central States Distributing Co., Indianapolis, Ind.
Words and Music by J. Owen Smith.
All rights reserved. All Mechanical and Preforming rights strictly reserved.
PRICE 50 CENTS

sometimes draped with electric lights. A sword represented the fight against the enemies of a Christian life. New initiates were sprinkled with water to purify them of foreign influences. The opening and closing prayers included the phrase, "The living Christ is a Klansman's criterion of character," and while the official Klan anthem was "The Fiery Cross," mainstream Christian

People and Their Place in Society

Dearly beloved, avenge not yourselves, but rather give place unto wrath: for it is written, Vengeance is mine; I will repay, saith the Lord. Therefore if thine enemy hunger, feed him; if he thirst, give him drink: for in so doing thou shalt heap coals of fire on his head. Be not overcome of evil, but overcome evil with good.
—Romans 12:19–21

For many walk, of whom I have told you often, and now tell you even weeping, that they are the enemies of the cross of Christ.
—Philippians 3:18

Detail of sheet music art for "Hurrah for the Ku Klux Klan" (Courtesy Library of Congress)

"Onward Ku Klux Klansmen"

"The Klan Is Watching You"

"In the Light of the Fiery Cross"

"A Prayer of a Klansman"

"The Klansman and the Pope"

"Take Up Thy Cross"

"Put the Bible Back into the Schools"

—Klan songs, sheet music, and piano rolls

hymns were also popular. "The Old Rugged Cross" and "Onward Christian Soldiers," were often included at rallies and parades.

Appropriation of the Bible and Christian symbols vary from group to group and region to region today. But it is the burning Cross for which the Klan is best known—spreading the light of their message as they turn the Cross into a symbol of suppression and terror. In other white supremacy groups, Bibles (and Adolf Hitler's *Mein Kampf)* are often found with caches of weapons, confiscated in law enforcement raids.

The Klan's original targets were blacks, then Catholics, immigrants, and Jews (only a decade before Hitler's rise to power). The civil rights movement of the 1950s and 1960s saw a renewed emphasis on blacks and their Jewish allies. Homosexuals and people with AIDS were added to the list in the '70s and '80s.

Today, estimated membership in the Klan is around ten thousand. But according to the watchdog group Klanwatch, 327 white supremacy groups exist in the U.S., varying in size from two people with a post office box to unknown thousands. Once a national fraternity often wielding the influence of a major political party, the Klan is now seen as fringe, with factionalized, regional groups. Many individuals have left, moving from the vigilante to the political, and into more mainstream groups. David Duke, a former Klansman and white supremacist who was "born again," was a Republican candidate for governor in Louisiana.

Night-riding (an early Klan practice in which hooded horsemen carried torches and burning crosses through the streets and countryside) has been replaced by the nightly news and talk shows as a means of expressing white supremacists' ideals; many feel their role has changed from that of enforcers to barometers, voicing the concerns of what they see as a majority of like-minded, native-born, white Protestants.

Many believe the millennium is at hand and that a "race war" between blacks and whites will precede the return of Christ. Charles Manson, among others, shares this view, based on the book of Revelation.

To Prove a Black Presence in the Bible

Most Christians in America can think of one non-white biblical character. He shows up every Christmas, lined up with the other two Wise Men in the nativity scene, on hand to worship the white, often blond and blue-eyed infant Jesus.

Western European tradition has generally segregated blacks and people of color in the Bible and throughout history, moving their roles and contributions into the background or omitting them completely.

On Good Friday, 1993, Archbishop George Augustus Stallings, Jr. of Washington, D.C., burned an image of a white Jesus in the street as he proclaimed its "historical inaccuracy": "Jesus was an 'Afro-Asiatic Jew.' "

In public schools, rather than Sunday schools, the Afrocentric movement has been most controversial. Afrocentrism's critics

Images of a black Jesus can be readily found in most areas with large black populations.

acknowledge that many historical truths have been left out of the various academic disciplines, but that much misinformation is disseminated by the movement, primarily to make people feel better

"God is a negro . . . the bulk of you and all the fool Negroes believe that God is a white-skinned, blue-eyed, straight-haired, projecting nosed, compressed lipped and finely robed *white* gentleman, sitting upon a throne in the heavens."

—Bishop Henry M. Turner, African Methodist Episcopal Church in the United States (1898)

And when the queen of Sheba heard of the fame of Solomon concerning the name of the Lord, she came to prove him with hard questions . . . And she said to the king, . . . Blessed be the Lord thy God, which delighted in thee, to set thee on the throne of Israel: because the Lord loved Israel for ever, therefore made he thee king, to do judgment and justice.
—I Kings 10:1–9 (excerpt)

And Miriam and Aaron spake against Moses because of the Ethiopian woman whom he had married: for he had married an Ethiopian woman.
—Numbers 12:1

Return, return, O Shulamite; return, return, that we may look upon thee. What will ye see in the Shulamite? As it were the company of two armies.
—Song of Solomon 6:13

14

"Solomon treated the Queen of Sheba, a negress of Abyssinia, with the utmost respect and cordiality; Philip ran reverently by the side of the chariot of a negro, the chief minister of the court of her successor; Moses married an Ethiopian; a negro was called of God and his brethren to be one of 'the prophets and teachers of the church at Antioch,' with Barnabas and the foster-brother of Herod, and was also called by the Holy Ghost to lay his hands, in company of those of his brethren, upon the heads of Paul and Barnabas—the first Christian ordination that is upon record, and one that our ministers would do well speedily to imitate."

—From a sermon first preached at Wilbraham, Massachusetts, in 1854 by the Reverend Gilbert Haven, Methodist Episcopal Church

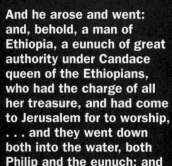

And he arose and went: and, behold, a man of Ethiopia, a eunuch of great authority under Candace queen of the Ethiopians, who had the charge of all her treasure, and had come to Jerusalem for to worship, . . . and they went down both into the water, both Philip and the eunuch; and he baptized him.
—Acts 8:27–38 (excerpt)

Now there were in the church that was at Antioch certain prophets and teachers; as Barnabas, and Simeon that was called Niger, and Lucius of Cyrene, and Manaen, which had been brought up with Herod the tetrarch, and Saul.
—Acts 13:1

about their own racial or ethnic backgrounds.

The Afrocentric history curriculum focuses on ancient Egypt as the cradle of civilization. The debate is concerned not with the accomplishments of the Egyptians and their neighbors, nor the fact that they thrived on the continent of Africa. It's about whether they can be described as black Africans.

The same challenge faces those who search for a black presence in the ancient world of the Bible.

One of the most illustrious visitors to the court of King Solomon was the Queen of Sheba (I Kings 10). She praised Solomon's wisdom and leadership and marveled

at the power of the God of Israel. Their meeting concluded with a lavish exchange of gifts, and she went back home.

But where was Sheba? Scholar and theologian Cain Hope Felder concluded that the Queen of Sheba was a black Ethiopian, although "the task of recovering

The ankh. This ancient Egyptian symbol of life often appears in the imagery of Afrocentric Christianity.

The Bible Tells Me So

> "You shouldn't dis the Almighty's name, using it in cuss words or rapping with one another. It ain't cool and payback's a monster."
>
> —One of the Ten Commandments as presented in *The Black Bible Chronicles* (1993), the Bible translated into street language by P. K. McCary

this Black biblical presence is thwarted by the racist or ethnocentric presuppositions of several influential Western scholars."

The very first Gentile convert (the Ethiopian Eunuch) may have been black (Acts 8:26–40). Simeon the Black (Niger) was one of the leaders of the church at Antioch (Acts 13:1). One of Moses' wives was black (Numbers 12:1).

Among strict Afrocentrics and those who are simply searching for the historical truth, there are wide differences of opinion over whether some specific biblical characters were black. Ultimately, the point is the degree to which black people can see themselves in Christ and the stories of the people in the Bible.

For most Christians, black or white, the first exposure to the Bible was through pictures, not words. And African-Americans have cherished Bibles illustrated with paintings by European Old

Masters and nineteenth-century French academic painters, peopled with European interpretations of biblical characters. Other than an occasional "Moorish" slave, there are few blacks. Arabs are cast as villains. In the twentieth century, the stars of the Bible have been portrayed by the stars of the Cleopatra. Afrocentrism focuses on the peoples of ancient Egypt and the accomplishments of African civilization.

Adam and Eve

Ishmael

Pharaoh's daughter (who rescued the infant Moses)

Moses

Goliath

Solomon

Queen of Sheba

Jezebel

Balthazar— the black magi from Sheba

Mary

Jesus

Simon the Apostle

Simon that was called Niger

The eunuch— first convert

Biblical characters variously defined or depicted as black, African, Ethiopian, Afro-Asian, and of African descent through marriage with other races. Over one hundred are said to fall into this general category.

16

Now when Ebedmelech the Ethiopian, one of the eunuchs which was in the king's house, heard that they had put Jeremiah in the dungeon; the king then sitting in the gate of Benjamin; Ebedmelech went forth out of the king's house, and spake to the king, saying, My lord the king, these men have done evil in all that they have done to Jeremiah the prophet, whom they have cast into the dungeon; and he is like to die for hunger in the place where he is: for there is no more bread in the city.

—Jeremiah 38:7–9

The black wise man. Detail of seventeenth-century Bible illustration of the magi before the infant Jesus.

"If they left you out of the history books, what makes you think they won't tamper with your Jesus?"

—Archbishop George Augustus Stallings, Jr., of Washington, D.C., who stood before a crowd on Easter Sunday and burned a picture of a white Jesus (1993)

day: Charlton Heston, Victor Mature, and Hedy Lamarr.

This reflects a logical, gradual visual incorporation of the Bible by the dominant culture. But it is, of course, historically incorrect, and could be entwined with other sensitive issues, such as questions of racial or cultural superiority. Without pressure for affirmative action, certainly, few biblical characters would have access to many American country clubs today—not even Jesus, a north African Jew.

Strict Afrocentrics startle fellow Christians with a "historically accurate" picture of the black Christ, along with their justifications for this racial resurrection. But it is neither the historic Jesus nor a Jesus claimed by a particular ethnic or racial group who has entered the lives of millions over the past two thousand years. It is the Jesus of faith, the universally available Christ—the itinerant preacher from Galilee who spoke of grace and salvation for all mankind.

Historians and archaeologists are making it clear that the racially diverse population of late-twentieth-century America has more in common with the original biblical cast of characters than was presented through European tradition.

The Ethiopian eunuch. A seventeenth-century engraving depicts the story of his baptism accounted in Acts 8.

The Bible Tells Me So

The Congress of Racial Equality marches in memory of the four little girls killed in the bombing of a Birmingham, Alabama, Baptist church. (Washington, D.C., 1963)

To Justify Civil Rights for African-Americans

The Bible, as a source of liberation imagery, played an integral role in the civil rights movement from its very beginnings: "All are equal in the eyes of God" (Galatians 3:28, Genesis 1:26–27).

"Negro spirituals" include many references to freedom—often to the Israelites' flight from captivity in Egypt, with the refrain "Let my people go."

The black church was an important political force within the black community, and inspired a number of prominent civil rights leaders who were intimate with Scripture. The prime example is Dr. Martin Luther King, Jr.

Dr. King's choice of vocabulary—which now might be referred to as "code words"—communicated imagery well known to Christians.

In reference to the case popularly known as *Brown* v. *The Board of Education* (1954), Dr. King saw his people as leaving "Egypt" and reaching the "promised land," adding that the Supreme Court had "opened the Red

And thou shalt say unto him, The Lord God of the Hebrews hath sent me unto thee, saying, Let my people go, that they may serve me in the wilderness . . .
—Exodus 7:16

For ye shall pass over Jordan to go in to possess the land which the Lord your God giveth you, and ye shall possess it, and dwell therein.
—Deuteronomy 11:31

And when Pharaoh saw that the rain and the hail and the thunders were ceased, he sinned yet more, and hardened his heart, he and his servants. And the heart of Pharaoh was hardened, neither would he let the children of Israel go; as the Lord had spoken by Moses.
—Exodus 9:34–35

He hath shewed thee, O man, what is good; and what doth the Lord require of thee, but to do justly, and to love mercy, and to walk humbly with thy God?
—Micah 6:8

I have raised him up in righteousness, and I will direct all his ways: he shall build my city, and he shall let go my captives, not for price nor reward, saith the Lord of hosts.
—Isaiah 45:13

"While these songs remain, the colored people, like the Jews of old, will remember that 'they were once the bondmen in Egypt; and then will they go their way with memory on the alert, lest a worse thing come unto them, singing as they go:

Brother, ain't you glad you've left that heatheren (sic) army;
Brotheren (sic), ain't you glad the sea give away.' "

—Marshall W. Taylor, D.D., in the preface to his *A Collection of Revival Hymns and Plantation Melodies* (1882)

Martin Luther King, Jr. at a press conference in Washington, D.C. (1964)

Sea." His 1963 speech at the Lincoln Memorial shows his belief that we, as a nation, could reach this promised land. And King labeled the proponents of slavery, segregation, and Jim Crow policy as "the pharaohs of the South."

Echoing the Bible further, he observed that we "see men as Jews or Gentiles, Catholics or Protestants, Chinese or American, Negroes or whites," but that we all share God's "divine image." To American Christians he said: ". . . God is neither Baptist, Methodist, Presbyterian, or Episcopalian. God transcends our denominations."

King also turned Scripture into a strategy for social change. In sharp contrast to the actions of his white opponents, King's most outstanding contribution to the civil rights movement was his incorporation of the nonviolence exemplified by Jesus, and the practice of true Christian love. To "love your enemies" was a big order to follow (see Matthew 5:39, Matthew 5:44,

Luke 6:27–28, Luke 6:29). Some men felt that truly practicing this level of Christian love was impossible. Many others fighting for racial equality apparently found it to be impractical, notably the more extremist elements of the Black Power Movement and The Nation of Islam.

During the battle for civil rights, King was in a minority of black clergymen, cautioning them that they were too caught up in the good "over yonder" and needed to deal with the here and now. King also showed the

And unto him that smiteth thee on the one cheek offer also the other . . .
—Luke 6:29

But I say unto you, Love your enemies, bless them that curse you, do good to them that hate you, and pray for them which despitefully use you, and persecute you.
—Matthew 5:44

But I say unto you which hear, Love your enemies, do good to them which hate you, Bless them that curse you, and pray for them which despitefully use you.
—Luke 6:27–28

The Bible Tells Me So

hypocrisy of white Christians who contributed to the perpetuation of racism and segregation—as many have pointed out, King used their religious vocabulary, which challenged American Christians to take up the debate in their own churches.

Today, religion has again been called into service for change, but by those who consider themselves to be a persecuted and ignored "majority" group. Stephen L. Carter, in *The Culture of Disbelief: How American Law and Politics Trivialize Religious Devotion,* states that "there is little about the civil rights movement, other than the vital distinction in the ends that it sought, that makes it very different from the right-wing religious movements of the present day."

Had Dr. King's use of the Bible occurred today, he would no doubt be embroiled in a controversy similar to that surrounding the 1992 Republican National Convention, in which the Republican Party allied itself with the biblically oriented religious right.

Yet, rather than declaring a "cultural war," as did some Republicans, King practiced nonviolent protest in the streets. Instead of using religious superiority to brand and exclude the perceived non-Christian "enemies of family values," he preached a gospel of inclusion.

Rather than being part of a wealthy, entrenched group with the resources and power to set the tone for a major political campaign, he spoke for a group that had no enforced constitutional rights, no right to vote, whose economic power could be exerted only by the simple act of boycotting a lunch counter or department store.

King believed that "The Church . . . is not the master or the servant of the state, but rather the conscience of the state. It must be the guide and the critic of the state, and never its tool."

There is neither Jew nor Greek, there is neither bond nor free, there is neither male nor female: for ye are all one in Christ Jesus.
—Galatians 3:28

And God said, Let us make man in our image, after our likeness . . . So God created man in his own image, in the image of God created he him; male and female created he them.
—Genesis 1:26–27

But I say unto you, That ye resist not evil: but whosoever shall smite thee on thy right cheek, turn to him the other also.
—Matthew 5:39

When Israel was in Egypt land,
Let my people go;
Oppressed so hard, they could
    not stand,
Let my people go.
Thus saith the Lord, bold Moses
    said,
Let my people go;
If not, I'll smite your first-born
    dead,
Let my people go.
Go down, Moses, 'way down in
    Egypt land.
Tell King Pharoah, to let my
    people go.

—"Go Down, Moses," an American
    Slave Spiritual (see Exodus 3:10)

19

"The New Testament reveals that Jews 'both killed the Lord Jesus and their own prophets, and have persecuted us; and they please not God, and are contrary to all men (I Thess. 2:15). History records the terrible sufferings the Jewish people have experienced as a result."

—From an editorial in Pat Robertson's Christian Coalition's newsletter, July/August 1991

Pilate saith unto them, What shall I do then with Jesus which is called Christ? They all [the Jews] say unto him, Let him be crucified . . . Then answered all the people, and said, His blood be on us, and on our children.
—Matthew 27:22, 25

Ye stiffnecked and uncircumcised in heart and ears, ye do always resist the Holy Ghost: as your fathers did, so do ye. Which of the prophets have not your fathers persecuted? and they have slain them which shewed before of the coming of the Just One; of whom ye have been now the betrayers and murderers.
—Acts 7:51–52

After these things Jesus walked in Galilee: for he would not walk in Jewry, because the Jews sought to kill him.
—John 7:1

To Persecute the Jews

Since the early days of Christianity, the Scriptures and their interpretation have been an important tool in the persecution of Jewish people.

Collectively held responsible for the crucifixion of Christ (Matthew 27:22 and 25, I Thessalonians 2:14–15), Jews are the only group of people to be accused of deicide—the killing of God. They made Jesus, one of their own, an outcast (John 7:1). They have been attacked for refusing to convert to Christianity (Acts 7:51–52). The Jews were pagans, a people damned to hell, accused of devil worship (in reference to John 8:44).

In the medieval Christian world, Jews were massacred after having been accused of causing plagues by poisoning water supplies, kidnapping Christian children in order to use their blood for rituals, and stealing consecrated communion bread to desecrate the body of Christ. Prime targets during the Spanish Inquisition, many Jews converted to Christianity, but were believed to practice Judaism in secret. These Jews were

"Don't ever argue with Christ. He's a Jew."

—Television evangelist Jimmy Swaggart

Star of David patch, circa 1940. In Nazi Germany, Jews were required to wear the patches, under threat of death, to identify their heritage.

known as "Marranos" (usually translated as "pigs"). Those who would not repent were executed publicly to maintain the purity of the "true faith." Public records during this time referred to those of mixed parentage as "half New Christians" or "three-quarters New Christians."

Jews were excluded from public office, frequently denied citizenship, forbidden to own property or to farm. In the twelfth century, Christians were forbidden to charge interest for lending money (Exodus 22:25, Deuteronomy 23:19). This nasty necessity was turned over to the Jews, who had few other means of earning a living. This left them open to persecu-

Jews of Cologne burned alive, from a nineteenth-century facsimile of a 1493 woodcut.

tion for yet another reason if their Christian clients thought the interest rates excessive.

Victims of pogroms or "ethnic cleansing," they faced continued bigotry upon their arrival in a new homeland, while myth and literature proclaimed the story of the wandering Jew (the "God-smiter" who cruelly rushed Jesus as he carried his cross), condemned to wander the Earth in repentance, exiled for a stubborn rejection of Christ.

While there were episodes of relative tranquillity over the centuries, anti-Semitism was a continual threat.

In this century, justification for anti-Semitism has been economic and "scientific." In the 1920s, Henry Ford expressed anti-Semitic views in his newspaper, the *Dearborn Independent.* He reprinted excerpts from *The Protocols of the Elders of Zion,* a bogus document containing minutes of a fictitious meeting of Jews intent on world domination. "Takeover" questions continued, with, for example, Nixon's alleged concern about a Jewish monopoly of the media, and a fear of the "Jewish element" of the ACLU, which, according to Billy McCormack, director of the Christian Coalition, is ". . . trying to drive Christianity out of the public place . . . the ACLU is made up of a tremendous amount of Jewish attorneys."

Under Hitler, the science of eugenics was on the side of anti-Semites. The Nazis built their anti-Semitism on a foundation of Aryan superiority and the inherent inferiority of the Jews. The Nazi Holocaust, in which six million Jews and other "undesirables" were systematically executed as part of government policy, was seen as the final solution to the "Jewish problem."

While much less threatening to

For ye, brethren, became followers of the churches of God which in Judaea are in Christ Jesus: for ye also have suffered like things of your own countrymen, even as they have of the Jews: Who both killed the Lord Jesus, and their own prophets, and have persecuted us; and they please not God, and are contrary to all men.
—I Thessalonians 2:14–15

Ye are of your father the devil, and the lusts of your father ye will do. He was a murderer from the beginning, and abode not in the truth, because there is no truth in him. When he speaketh a lie, he speaketh of his own: for he is a liar, and the father of it.
—John 8:44 (words spoken by Jesus when reminded by the Jews that Abraham is their father)

21

"Let him be crucified!" (Matthew 27:22, 23) A seventeenth-century engraving depicting Christ before the Jews.

"Your sect [Judaism] by its sufferings has furnished a remarkable proof of the universal spirit of religious intolerance inherent in every sect, disclaimed by all while feeble, and practiced by all when in power."
—Thomas Jefferson (1818)

[Turn in to the Inquisition authorities people who] observe the Sabbath, putting on clean or festive clothes, clean and washed shirts . . . arranging and cleaning their houses on Friday afternoon, and in the evening lighting new candles . . . cooking on the said Fridays such food as is required for the Saturday . . . cleansing, or causing meat to be cleaned, cutting away from it all fat and grease, . . . not eating pork, hare, rabbit, strangled birds, conger-eel, cuttlefish, nor eels or other scaleless fish, as laid down by Jewish law . . . give Old Testament names to children . . . who say that the dead Law of Moses is good. . . ."

—As quoted by Cecil Roth in *A History of the Marranos* (1932)

Illustration depicting the rumor of Jews calling the Devil from a vessel of blood. In addition to a reference to Jews and the Devil in John 8:44, a second-century mistranslation concerning Moses' descent from Mt. Sinai confused the Hebrew *karan* ("was radiant") with *keren* ("horn"): thus, Moses' face "was horned" ("*cornuta esset*"). Further evidence of this tradition can be seen in Michaelangelo's sculpture "Moses," which depicts "horns."

personal safety, anti-Semitism on the American scene has a long, complex history, including the activities of the Ku Klux Klan. Jews had their time as targets of anti-immigration movements, as have Catholics and other religious and ethnic groups. There were quotas for Jewish students in universities. Jews were barred from certain hotels and other public accommodations well into the '50s and '60s.

More recently, The Nation of Islam has spread the word of a Jewish threat and a supposed history of Jewish evil toward black people. Jews, they claim, are primarily responsible for the entire slave trade and instrumental in depriving blacks of economic success and power. Yet many Jews and blacks are initiating dialogues and forming new alliances. In some cities, blacks have been invited to participate in Passover observances, acknowledging their common history of ancestors who were delivered from bondage in slavery.

Self-proclaimed historians and scholars who deny the existence of the Holocaust protested the opening of the Holocaust Museum in Washington, D.C., in 1993. Gas, they said, was for delousing. Piles of shoes at concentration camps were actually a recycling project. The myth of the Holocaust, they argued, was perpetuated to gain support for a state of Israel, or some international Jewish conspiracy.

There have been some reversals in the age-old trend toward anti-Semitism, however. In 1961, the World Council of Churches condemned anti-Semitism as incompatible with the teachings of Christ. In 1962, during the Second Vatican Council, the words "perfidious Jews"—the treacherous traitors of Christ—were deleted from Catholics' Good Friday worship. In

"What then shall we Christians do with this damned, rejected race of Jews?

First, their synagogues or churches should be set on fire, . . .

Secondly, their homes should likewise be broken down and destroyed . . . They ought to be put under one roof or in a stable, like gypsies.

Thirdly, they should be deprived of their prayer-books and Talmuds in which such idolatry, lies, cursing, and blasphemy are taught.

Fourthly, their rabbis must be forbidden under threat of death to teach any more . . .

Fifthly, passport and travelling privileges should be absolutely forbidden to the Jews . . .

Sixthly, they ought to be stopped from usury. All their cash and valuables of silver and gold ought to be taken from them and put aside for safe keeping . . .

Seventhly, let the young and strong Jews and Jewesses be given the flail, the axe, the hoe, the spade, the distaff, and spindle, and let them earn their bread by the sweat of their noses as is enjoined upon Adam's children . . .

. . . To sum up, dear princes and nobles who have Jews in your domains, if this advice of mine does not suit you, then find a better one so that you and we may all be free of this unsufferable devilish burden—the Jews."

—Martin Luther, upset over the reluctance of Jews to convert to Christianity (1543)

Reverend Fr. Charles E. Coughlin, Irish-Catholic priest and vocal anti-communist, and one of the first clergymen to use broadcasting (radio) as a powerful political tool. In the 1930s, radio audiences heard him rail against the threat of Jews to America's economy and defend Hitler's treatment of Jews as justified in the fight against communism. American Catholic officials were appalled. Coughlin published excerpts of "The Elders of Zion" in his magazine *Social Justice.*

1965, The Vatican reconsidered and rejected the idea of collective Jewish guilt for the death of Jesus. In April 1994, a Holocaust memorial ceremony was held in Vatican City, marking the first official Vatican recognition of the Holocaust. A month later, full diplomatic relations were established between the Vatican and Israel.

Leaders of the 5.2 million-member Evangelical Lutheran Church in America drafted a declaration in 1994 that repudiated founder Martin Luther's anti-Semitic writings, acknowledging the use of these writings by Nazis and other anti-Semites and pledging "to oppose the deadly workings of anti-Semitism in church and society."

"We trust that the Gentiles will not entertain feelings of hatred against the erroneously believing mass of Israel in its innocence of the Satanic sin of its leaders—the Scribes and Pharisees—who have already once proved themselves to be the destruction of Israel. . . ."

—Anonymous introduction to a 1920 English edition of *The Jewish Peril: Protocols of the Learned Elders of Zion,* as published by "The Britons"

> Unto the woman he said, I will greatly multiply thy sorrow and thy conception; in sorrow thou shalt bring forth children; and thy desire shall be to thy husband, and he shall rule over thee.
>
> —Genesis 3:16

> But I suffer not a woman to teach, nor to usurp authority over the man, but to be in silence. For Adam was first formed, then Eve. And Adam was not deceived, but the woman being deceived was in the transgression. Notwithstanding she shall be saved in childbearing, if they continue in faith and charity and holiness with sobriety.
>
> —I Timothy 2:12–15

> But I would have you know, that the head of every man is Christ; and the head of the woman is the man; and the head of Christ is God.
>
> —I Corinthians 11:3

> Wives, submit yourselves unto your own husbands, as unto the Lord. For the husband is the head of the wife, even as Christ is the head of the church: and he is the saviour of the body. Therefore as the church is subject unto Christ, so let the wives be to their own husbands in every thing.
>
> —Ephesians 5:22–24

"The Birth of Eve." In this fifteenth-century woodcut, God oversees Eve's delivery from the side of the sleeping Adam.

To Define the Traditional Role of Women

In a very literal reading of the Bible, women must live by the guidelines presented to "man" or "mankind," as well as a number of additional rules and regulations specifically for and about them. In the book of Genesis, women are blamed for the fall of mankind and are "cursed" to bear children.

The Old Testament contains instruction regarding female behavior, obedience to the husband, and menstruation and cleanliness. Women were often considered untouchable, especially during menstruation and after the birth of a child; giving birth to a female doubled the time in which a mother would be "unclean."

Women were considered to rival the Devil as the greatest source of temptation and influence over men. Beware of a Delilah or a Jezebel. An ultimate warning is found in Ecclesiastes 7:26: "And I find more bitter than death the woman, whose heart is snares and nets, and her hands as bands: whoso pleaseth God shall escape from her; but the sinner shall be taken by her."

Many of the old laws pertaining to women are lifted in the New Testament. Women became equals in the eyes of Christ but not in those of their Christian brethren. New Testament authors, particularly Paul, devised more regulations; many still have bearing on women's lives today, both inside and outside the church.

Nowhere in the Bible is it stated that women are allowed leadership in politics or worship except

> "American women are also especially fortunate to be the beneficiaries of the Judeo-Christian tradition, which affords a status to women unknown in the rest of the world."
>
> —Anti-ERA crusader Phyllis Schlafly (1978)

"Tell him he is mistaken. If he will turn to 2 Chron. xxxiv.22, he will find that when Josiah, the king, sent the wise men to consult Huldah, the prophetess, about the book of laws . . . they found Huldah in the college in Jerusalem, thoroughly well informed on questions of state, while Shallum, her husband, was keeper of the robes. I suppose his business was to sew on the royal buttons."

—Elizabeth Cady Stanton in reply to a wealthy woman who stated that she could not contribute to a women's college because her minister told her that there was nothing in the Bible about colleges for women. The woman was not impressed and gave thirty thousand dollars to Princeton.

Elizabeth Cady Stanton (1815–1902), founder and first president of the National Woman Suffrage Association, and author/editor of *The Woman's Bible.* Pictured here with her daughter, Harriot, in 1856.

in "extreme" circumstances, such as those of Miriam and Deborah in the Old Testament and Priscilla in the New Testament. The Bible has been interpreted to inform women of their "special" role, primarily within the family. They can stay on their pedestal or step off, risking eternal damnation.

In nineteenth-century America, a movement began to challenge male hierarchy, with the Bible as primary ammunition. Biblical interpretation had been key to keeping women in their place; now it would be used to free them.

One of the most prominent, burning issues for these activists

People and Their Place in Society

Let your women keep silence in the churches: for it is not permitted unto them to speak; but they are commanded to be under obedience, as also saith the law. And if they will learn any thing, let them ask their husbands at home: for it is a shame for women to speak in the church.
—I Corinthians 14:34–35

Also thou shalt not approach unto a woman to uncover her nakedness, as long as she is put apart for her uncleanness.
—Leviticus 18:19

> And if a woman have an issue, and her issue in her flesh be blood, she shall be put apart seven days: and whosoever toucheth her shall be unclean until the even. And every thing that she lieth upon in her separation shall be unclean: every thing also that she sitteth upon shall be unclean. And whosoever toucheth her bed shall wash his clothes, and bathe himself in water, and be unclean until the even.
>
> —Leviticus 15:19–21

> But speak thou the things which become sound doctrine: . . . The aged women likewise, that they be in behaviour as becometh holiness . . . To be discreet, chaste, keepers at home, good, obedient to their own husbands, that the word of God be not blasphemed.
>
> —Titus 2:1,3,5

"THE CURSE"

A popular term for menstruation, part of the "sorrow" of a woman's childbearing years as decreed by God (Genesis 3:16). In the Bible also known as the "custom of women" (Genesis 31:35). Strict taboos are recorded in Leviticus. The cloth used in ancient days for feminine hygiene was a symbol of ultimate filth (Isaiah 30:22).

concerned whether women should be allowed to vote. In 1840, abolitionist Elizabeth Cady Stanton and eight other prominent women were locked out of an anti-slavery convention in England. While actively involved in the fights for prison reform, abolishment of slavery, and the anti-alcohol movement, they were not allowed to participate on an equal basis with men.

In retaliation, the women spearheaded the *Seneca Falls Declaration of Sentiments and Resolutions of 1848,* the first document of the feminist movement in the United States:

"The history of mankind is a history of repeated injuries and usurpations on the part of man toward woman. . . . He allows her in Church, as well as State, but a subordinate position, claiming Apostolic authority for her exclusion from the ministry, and, with some exceptions, from any public participation in the affairs of the Church . . . He has created . . . a different code of morals for men and women . . . we insist that [women] have immediate admission to all the rights and privileges which belong to them as citizens of the United States . . . woman is man's equal—was intended to be so by the Creator . . . woman has too long rested satisfied in the cir-

cumscribed limits which corrupt customs and a perverted application of the Scriptures have marked out for her, and that it is time she should move in the enlarged sphere which her great Creator has assigned her."

The resolutions received the unanimous approval of the over one hundred Seneca Falls Convention attendees, with one exception: the right of women to vote. Abolitionist Frederick Douglass, himself denied equality because he was black, joined Stanton in casting a key vote for women's suffrage.

The Woman's Bible was completed in 1895. Most of the arguments used in issues during the next century—from suffrage through the Equal Rights Amend-

> "The woman is not designed by God, nor entitled to all the franchises in society to which the male is entitled . . . God has disqualified her for any such exercise of them as would benefit herself or society, by the endowments of body, mind, and heart he has given her, and the share he has assigned her in the tasks of social existence."
>
> —Reverend R. L. Dabney in response to the idea of women in the pulpit (1879)

The woman voter could gain too much power: this one is leaving her husband at home to tend to the children (1909).

As an eagle stirreth up her nest, fluttereth over her young, spreadeth abroad her wings, taketh them, beareth them on her wings: So the Lord alone did lead him, and there was no strange god with him.

—Deuteronomy 32:11–12, one of several verses referring to God using feminine imagery

It is better to dwell in the wilderness, than with a contentious and an angry woman.

—Proverbs 21:19

Speak unto the children of Israel, saying, If a woman have conceived seed, and born a man child: then she shall be unclean seven days; according to the days of the separation for her infirmity shall she be unclean . . . But if she bear a maid child, then she shall be unclean two weeks, as in her separation: and she shall continue in the blood of her purifying threescore and six days.

—Leviticus 12:2, 5

ment, the ordination of women, and the restoration of "family values"—can be found in this book.

In the introduction, Stanton states that ". . . political parties and religious denominations have alike taught that woman was made after man, of man, and for man, an inferior being, subject to man . . ."

To create *The Woman's Bible,* over twenty women bought two Bibles apiece, cut out Scriptures pertaining to women, and pasted them to pieces of paper on which they wrote their own Scriptural interpretations from a woman's perspective.

Not surprisingly, the resulting "Bible" was not roundly accepted: "You might as well have a 'Shoe-makers' Bible," said one minister. Another called it ". . . the work of women, and the devil."

One of America's Founding Fathers, Thomas Jefferson (1743-1826), did precisely the same thing—using scissors, he re-arranged the passages of the Bible into his vision of the essential message of Jesus.

Elizabeth Cady Stanton died in 1902, eighteen years before women attained the right to vote.

"Seeing that the religious superstitions of women perpetuate their bondage more than all other adverse influences, I feel impelled to reiterate my demands for justice, liberty, and equality in the Church as well as in the State."

—Elizabeth Cady Stanton in *Eighty Years and More: Reminiscences 1815–1897*

28

"Give me your tired, your poor,
Your huddled masses yearning to
breathe free,
The wretched refuse of your teeming
shore,
Send these, the homeless, tempest-
tost to me:
I lift my lamp beside the golden door."

—Inscription, the Statue of Liberty,
New York, for over a century a symbol
of welcome to refugees seeking a
new life in the United States

Let brotherly love continue.
Be not forgetful to entertain
strangers: for thereby some
have entertained angels
unawares. Remember them
that are in bonds, as bound
with them; and them which
suffer adversity, as being
yourselves also in the body.
—Hebrews 13:1–3

Thus saith the Lord;
Execute ye judgment and
righteousness, and deliver
the spoiled out of the hand
of the oppressor: and do no
wrong, do no violence to the
stranger, the fatherless, nor
the widow, neither shed
innocent blood in this place.
—Jeremiah 22:3

The Lord executeth
righteousness and judgment
for all that are oppressed.
—Psalm 103:6

To Provide Sanctuary to Political Refugees

Christianity has long held a tradition of the "right of sanctuary," in
which the church has sheltered
those sought by political enemies
or accused of crimes. In the calm-
ness of a holy place, they could
search their souls and examine
their options.

During World War II, Christians in
America, Germany, and across
Europe helped Jews by hiding them
or arranging their escape from the
Nazis. With the onset of violence in
Central America in the '70s and
'80s, the tradition was extended
by Americans. Congregations—
Catholic, Protestant, and Jewish—
gave protection to political
refugees from El Salvador and
Guatemala, where wars resulted in
the dislocation, death, or "disap-
pearance" of tens of thousands by
military regimes. Refugees fled
interrogation, rape, torture, and
death, often for such crimes as participation in peaceful protest,
membership in labor unions, or
suspect religious affiliations. Many
of their cases were documented
by the United Nations High Commission for Refugees.

In the same way escaped slaves
were helped to the North over a
hundred years earlier, a new Underground Railroad evolved: once in
the United States, refugees were
fed, clothed, and sheltered by a
growing secret network of earnest
Americans. These refugees were
given a chance to tell their stories
of persecution, possibly embarrass-
ing the United States government
as it became more formally and
secretly involved in Central American politics and conflicts.

The congregations, from Catholics in Milwaukee to Baptists in
Seattle and Presbyterians in Tucson,
defied the federal government and
the Immigration and Naturalization
Service, which sought to deport the
refugees. The words of the Bible
provided justification by command-

1-800-LEV-1933

A trial information hotline number
set up during prosecution of
sanctuary workers, referring to
Leviticus 19:33

"Interior of the Cathedral at Bourges"
by Pierre Gaston Rigaud (1920). Oil on
panel.

ing hospitality to the stranger: "thou shalt love him as thyself" (Leviticus 19:34); "for ye were strangers in the land of Egypt" (Exodus 22:21). God's people and his community on earth were to be a "shelter" and "refuge and fortress" (Psalm 91:1–2).

Members of the movement argued that they were simply following their religious beliefs. For the government to forbid them the right to harbor refugees infringed on their constitutional right to freedom of religion.

The Reagan Administration determined that these were economic refugees (as opposed to political) and systematically enforced its policy of deportation and prosecution of those working in the sanctuary movement. As abolitionists in this country had defied the fugitive-slave laws over a century before, those providing sanctuary also answered to a higher power.

Is not this the fast that I have chosen? to loose the bands of wickedness, to undo the heavy burdens, and to let the oppressed go free, and that ye break every yoke? Is it not to deal thy bread to the hungry, and that thou bring the poor that are cast out to thy house? when thou seest the naked, that thou cover him; and that thou hide not thyself from thine own flesh?
—Isaiah 58:6–7

But whoso hath this world's good, and seeth his brother have need, and shutteth up his bowels of compassion from him, how dwelleth the love of God in him?
—I John 3:17

For we wrestle not against flesh and blood, but against principalities, against powers, against the rulers of the darkness of this world, against spiritual wickedness in high places.
—Ephesians 6:12

And if a stranger sojourn with thee in your land, ye shall not vex him. But the stranger that dwelleth with you shall be unto you as one born among you, and thou shalt love him as thyself; for ye were strangers in the land of Egypt: I am the Lord your God.
—Leviticus 19:33–34

" . . . For me, this declaration of sanctuary represents what Isaiah 58 tells us, that today you are sharing your bread with me, but even more importantly, you are helping to break the yoke of repression that binds the Salvadoran people. . . ."

—Testimony of René Sanchez, a victim of torture and persecution, in a Declaration of Public Sanctuary at All Souls Church, Unitarian (Washington, D.C., October 6, 1985)

People and Their Place in Society

I know that the Lord will maintain the cause of the afflicted, and the right of the poor.

—Psalm 140:12

For ye know the grace of our Lord Jesus Christ, that, though he was rich, yet for your sakes he became poor, that ye through his poverty might be rich.

—II Corinthians 8:9

And again I say unto you, it is easier for a camel to go through the eye of a needle, than for a rich man to enter into the kingdom of God.

—Matthew 19:24

Roadside shrine, Calderon, Ecuador

Cross reproduced in a style typical of Latin American religious art.

To Empower and Liberate the Poor

In liberation theology, God is experienced through the suffering and struggles of the poor. For many impoverished Latin American Catholics, this is an attempt to read the Bible from their perspective, as opposed to the Church's traditional reaction to the poor (passivity and accepting one's lot in life). Liberation theology promotes Christian activism, which often leads into the political arena.

Gustavo Gutiérrez, a Peruvian priest, developed the idea of *teología de la liberación.* In practice, thousands of Peruvian base communities bring groups of the poor together for Bible study and work to fulfill parishioners' basic needs, such as clean water and sewers. Priests, nuns, and lay leaders work with peasants to encourage spiritual growth and vision using specific passages of Scripture. There is a focus on God's concern for liberation (Exodus 3:7–8). Latin American peoples recognize generals and wealthy landholders, in Micah 2:2 and Amos 8:5–6, as "you who trample upon the needy and destroy the poor of the land . . ."

The ministry of Jesus was among the poor and the outcast. Jesus practiced the ultimate charity (II Corinthians 8:9) and upset the status quo, the "business as usual" in the temples and among the established leaders.

The poor find themselves in the Bible, as the focus of Christ's ministry. Christianity rises up from their community of faith rather

". . . there's only one Gospel— the one that calls men and women to justice."

—Archbishop Desmond Tutu of South Africa (1994)

The Bible Tells Me So

The parable of the widow's mite (Luke 21), an example in the words of Jesus of the worth, contribution, and sincerity of the poor

than trickling down from rich and powerful oppressors or the authority of the Vatican.

With the fall of communism, many have expressed the view that liberation theology may no longer be viewed superficially as an international Marxist conspiracy, but as an empowering grassroots movement for millions of poor in the Third World.

In the United States, debate rages over the government's responsibility toward the poor. As reforms in welfare and related health and nutrition programs take hold, the church may find itself with a far more politically active role in the care and concerns of poor Americans.

"Poverty is not caused by fate; it is caused by the actions of those whom the prophet condemns: [Amos 2:6–7] . . . There are poor because some people are victims of others [Isaiah 10:1–2] . . . The prophets condemn every kind of abuse, every form of keeping the poor in poverty or of creating new poor people . . . In the New Testament oppression by the rich is also condemned (Luke 6:24–25; 12:13–21; 16:19–31; 18:18–26) and in the Letter of James (2:5–9; 4:13–17; 5:16) . . . The Bible speaks of positive and concrete measures to prevent poverty from becoming established among the People of God."

—Gustavo Gutiérrez in *A Theology of Liberation: History, Politics and Salvation* (1971)

And they covet fields, and take them by violence; and houses, and take them away: so they oppress a man and his house, even a man and his heritage.
—Micah 2:2

What mean ye that ye beat my people to pieces, and grind the faces of the poor? saith the Lord God of hosts.
—Isaiah 3:15

He that oppresseth the poor reproacheth his Maker: but he that honoureth him hath mercy on the poor.
—Proverbs 14:31

Rob not the poor, because he is poor: neither oppress the afflicted in the gate: For the Lord will plead their cause, and spoil the soul of those that spoiled them.
—Proverbs 22:22–23

Charge them that are rich in this world, that they be not highminded, nor trust in uncertain riches, but in the living God, who giveth us richly all things to enjoy; That they do good, that they be rich in good works, ready to distribute, willing to communicate; Laying up in store for themselves a good foundation against the time to come, that they may lay hold on eternal life.
—I Timothy 6:17–19

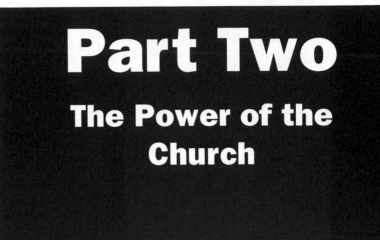

Part Two

The Power of the Church

Even so ye also outwardly appear righteous unto men; but within ye are full of hypocrisy and iniquity.

—Matthew 23:28

And when they shall say unto you, Seek unto them that have familiar spirits, and unto wizards that peep, and that mutter: should not a people seek unto their God? for the living to the dead? To the law and to the testimony: if they speak not according to this word, it is because there is no light in them.

—Isaiah 8:19–20

Thou shalt not suffer a witch to live.

—Exodus 22:18

Regard not them that have familiar spirits, neither seek after wizards, to be defiled by them: I am the Lord your God.

—Leviticus 19:31

And the soul that turneth after such as have familiar spirits, and after wizards, to go a whoring after them, I will even set my face against that soul, and will cut him off from among his people.

—Leviticus 20:6

S-A-N-T-A anagram for S-A-T-A-N.

—Anonymous source, quoted by satirists and writers such as Dana Carvey and David Sedaris

A old crone, her broom in hand, weaves the web of fate in this sixteenth-century engraving. In the 1960s, controversy erupted over the television program *Bewitched,* which portrayed a witch as an attractive housewife. Witchcraft is associated with satanism, leading to the current uproar over the observance of Halloween by children, particularly in public schools.

To Accuse and Execute Women as Witches

Every society has always had folk healers, mediums, specialists in herbal medicines and fertility problems, astrologers, and fortune-tellers. And every society has found groups to persecute: gypsies have a reputation as fortune-tellers with many occult traditions, and Jews have often been accused of satanic acts.

For several centuries, Christian authorities designated an enemy of the church at large in the general population: witches. Their existence was unquestioned, and the Bible warned against them. Midwives, women who never married, women who lived "in sin" with men, women who owned property or businesses, and women who challenged male authority were often accused of witchcraft. They had to be punished, along with heretics, nonbelievers, and nonconformists.

By the turn of the eighteenth

century, an estimated 300,000 "witches," mostly women, had been imprisoned, tortured, and put to death both in Europe and the New World.

King James I, who had the Bible translated into what has been the most enduring version, had a fascination with the occult. His version of the Bible replaced the Hebrew and Greek terms for *sorcerer (diviners* and *prophets)* with *witch.* Traditional European witches were quite different from those mentioned in the Bible.

The Witch's Hammer, an official document eventually sanctioned by the Vatican, came into wide use in the late 1500s. The *Hammer* and other guidelines included specifications for finding witches, tortures designed to exact confessions, procedures for sentencing, and means of execution.

Inquisitors had many techniques to identify witches. The test of throwing the accused into a body of water (if she drowned, she was innocent) was one used for determining guilt. Suspected witches were stripped to search for extra breasts (resembling warts) hidden on their bodies.

In New England, witchcraft was a felony (punishable by hanging), rather than heresy (which called for burning at the stake). The wicked witch was used as a threat

"The Witch's Hammer." Frontispiece of the *Malleus Malificarum* (circa 1500).

against disobedient children and became a prominent character in fairy tales.

The Old Testament warns against fortune-telling, casting spells, and seeking advice from the dead. Yet fortune-telling—considered one of the prime activities of witchcraft—is now routine. The daily horoscope is found in almost every newspaper in the country, in some cases right next to Ann Landers, Erma Bombeck, or Billy Graham's "My Answer." First Lady Nancy Reagan allegedly retained astrologers to determine ideal times for her husband's meetings

"After God Himself hath spoken of magicians and sorcerers, what infidel dare doubt that they exist?"

—Pierre de Lancre (1622)

A man also or woman that hath a familiar spirit, or that is a wizard, shall surely be put to death: they shall stone them with stones: their blood shall be upon them.

—Leviticus 20:27

There shall not be found among you any one that maketh his son or his daughter to pass through the fire, or that useth divination, or an observer of times, or an enchanter, or a witch, or a charmer, or a consulter with familiar spirits, or a wizard, or a necromancer.

—Deuteronomy 18:10–11

Thou art wearied in the multitude of thy counsels. Let now the astrologers, the stargazers, the monthly prognosticators, stand up, and save thee from these things that shall come upon thee.

—Isaiah 47:13

The Power of the Church

"The feminist agenda is not about equal rights for women . . . It is about a socialist, anti-family political movement that encourages women to leave their husbands, kill their children, practice witchcraft, destroy capitalism, and become Lesbians."

—Televangelist Pat Robertson
(1992)

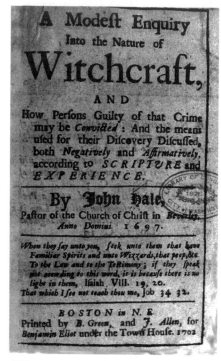

Title page of "A Modest Inquiry Into the Nature of Witchcraft . . ." by Reverend John Hale, 1697 (printed 1702), which includes an account of the Salem case.

and, consequently, his business of running the country.

Arthur Miller's 1953 Pulitzer prize–winning play *The Crucible* raised issues providing a direct parallel to the search for and persecution of communists and communist sympathizers, initiated by Republican Senator Joseph McCarthy. The 1960s television show *Bewitched* prompted outrage from the church for its portrayal of a witch as an attractive housewife. Halloween festivities for children have been discouraged by many because of the holiday's supernatural themes. And three centuries after the Salem witch trials, television evangelist Pat Robertson, CEO of CBN Television and The Family Channel and a one-time Republican candidate for president, sent out a fund-raising letter opposing the Equal Rights Amendment. His reasoning? Witchcraft, among other things.

While undertaking a "witch-hunt" has come to mean searching out and harassing those (such as political opponents) with unpopular views, the Robertson letter to supporters of his Christian Coalition brilliantly evoked both the new metaphorical meaning and its ancient use: to sound the alarm on a threatening, ungodly foe. And, by implication, all those who supported this evil amendment.

Title page of the *Malleus Malificarum* ("The Witch's Hammer"), circa 1500.

"Jesus and the Woman of Samaria" by Gustave Doré (John 4)

SUPPORT:
The woman then left her waterpot, and went her way into the city, and saith to the men, Come, see a man, which told me all things that ever I did: is not this the Christ?

—John 4:28–29

There is neither Jew nor Greek, there is neither bond nor free, there is neither male nor female: for ye are all one in Christ Jesus.

—Galatians 3:28

It was Mary Magdalene, and Joanna, and Mary the mother of James, and other women that were with them, which told these things unto the apostles.

—Luke 24:10

To Support or Oppose the Ordination of Women

The Samaritan woman gave Jesus a drink from the well. When she learned that He was the Messiah, she ran into the city, exclaiming, ". . . is this not the Christ?" (John 4:28–29). Perhaps this made her the first Christian preacher.

Yet "you cannot impose upon people as a matter of faith things that are not clearly proved in the scripture and consistent with the traditions of the Church," according to Reverend Geoffrey Kirk, an activist opposing the ordination of women in the Church of England.

In the early days of Christianity, priestesses were always associated with pagan religions. The Roman Catholic Church has supported the

"After she's convinced of what He says, she goes out . . . into the town and she tells the people what she has seen and heard and she proclaims, 'Is this the Christ?' If you believe preaching is proclaiming, then she was the first preacher."

—Reverend Cheryl Jordan, Kessler Park United Methodist Church, Dallas (1992)

In April 1994, the Vatican announced that females could become altar servers. Traditionally a role for boys, altar service often leads to the priesthood. For young girls, it was emphasized that this would not be the case.

OPPOSE:
I will therefore that men pray every where, lifting up holy hands, without wrath and doubting.

—I Timothy 2:8

Let the woman learn in silence with all subjection. But I suffer not a woman to teach, nor to usurp authority over the man, but to be in silence.

—I Timothy 2:11–12

But I would have you know, that the head of every man is Christ; and the head of the woman is the man; and the head of Christ is God . . . For a man indeed ought not to cover his head, forasmuch as he is the image and glory of God: but the woman is the glory of the man. For the man is not of the woman; but the woman of the man. Neither was the man created for the woman; but the woman for the man.

—I Corinthians 11:3, 7–9

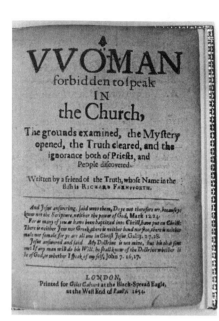

"Woman forbidden to speak in Church, The grounds examined, the Mystery opened, the Truth cleared, and the ignorance both of Priests, and People discovered . . ." Title page features Mark 12:24; Galatians 3:27, 28; and John 7:16, 17. (London, 1654)

exclusion of women from the priesthood for centuries. The Southern Baptist Convention, National Baptist Conventions, Church of God in Christ, Mormons, and part of the Episcopal Church and some other Protestant denominations still oppose or discourage the ordination of women, excluding more than half of all Christians from the clergy in the process.

For many, the contradictions of the Apostle Paul are at the core of any argument based on Scripture. Paul's biblical guidelines for women, both in church and in their relationships with men, reflect Jewish or local traditions. Yet Paul was impressed with several women in the growing congregations, commending Priscilla along with her husband, Aquila: they "risked their necks to save my life" (Romans 16:1–5). Paul differentiated Priscilla from other women, referring to her as "a fellow Apostle and fellow-bishop . . . [Paul] commends Phoebe, a Greek woman, as a minister (diakonos), which . . . may be legitimately interpreted as either presbyter, bishop, or Apostle," according to suffragette Elizabeth Cady Stanton in *The Woman's Bible* (1895), which speculates that Priscilla and Aquila founded the Church of Rome.

Catholics argue against women in the priesthood based on the model of the Mass, where the priest represents Jesus. But, while Jesus was indeed male, his importance for many is based on the fact that He became a human being, and all members of the human race are equal in His eyes.

Opponents also rely on the fact that Jesus chose no female apostles. Even Mary, His mother, was excluded. Wouldn't she have been the ideal candidate if women had been intended to lead?

The Bible Tells Me So

A Quaker woman speaking in Sunday meeting.

"There is strong reason to believe that the Apostle Priscilla, in co-operation with Aquila, performed the important task of founding the Church of Rome . . . [leading to the present] Roman Catholic Church, which would profit much by more remembrance and imitation of the modest and undogmatic women who helped to give it being and who nursed it through its infancy."

—Ellen Battelle Dietrick, contributor to *The Woman's Bible* (1895)

Women played important roles in the life of Jesus, as well as in the early life of the Church. And women were the first to bring the news of Christ's victory over death (Luke 24:10). Yet those who spread the word of Christ, the cornerstone of Christianity, are deemed unworthy of the pulpit by many Christian leaders.

Some refer to the debate as the Second Reformation. For many women, it is the issue that focuses on how they see themselves within their religious community; it heightens their concern about a male hierarchy that holds influence over public opinion and public policy affecting all women.

Right: "Women Speaking . . . Justified, Proved and Allowed of by the Scriptures, . . ." written in prison by Quaker Margaret Fell, 1666. This title page includes Acts 2:27, Joel 2:28, John 6:45, Isaiah 54:13, and Jeremiah 31:34. *The Quaker Collection, Haverford College Library.*

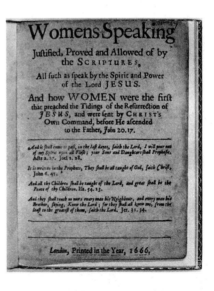

The Power of the Church

"To please his father, vex the Pope, and spite the devil."

—The reasons Martin Luther is said to have given for getting married

OPPOSE:
Now concerning the things whereof ye wrote unto me: It is good for a man not to touch a woman.
—I Corinthians 7:1

Now concerning virgins I have no commandment of the Lord: yet I give my judgment, as one that hath obtained mercy of the Lord to be faithful. I suppose therefore that this is good for the present distress, I say, that it is good for a man so to be.
—I Corinthians 7:25–26

His disciples say unto him, If the case of the man be so with his wife, it is not good to marry.
—Matthew 19:10

For there are some eunuchs, which were so born from their mother's womb: and there are some eunuchs, which were made eunuchs of men: and there be eunuchs, which have made themselves eunuchs for the kingdom of heaven's sake. He that is able to receive it, let him receive it.
—Matthew 19:12

To Support or Oppose the Marriage of Priests

The issue of optional celibacy for priests is an indicator, along with issues of birth control and the ordination of women, of division within the Catholic Church.

In 1054, with the split from the Church of Rome, Eastern Orthodox priests were allowed to marry (their bishops were not). With the Reformation came the Protestant perspective that marriage was a natural state for all men, including men of God.

The issue also illuminates one of the most obvious differences between Catholics and Protestants: there is no absolute biblical injunction that all men who have committed their lives to serving God and spreading His Word should be unmarried. Reformer Martin Luther was particularly fond of reciting I Timothy 4:1-5, celibacy being a refutation of the biblical injunction to "be fruitful and multiply." The reformed bachelor married and shared a former Augustinian monastery with a former nun.

The debate within the Catholic Church is complicated by the pronouncements of theologians and popes. Those in favor of marriage for priests turn to the Scriptures,

A priest officiates a wedding ceremony.

which can be interpreted as disapproving the tradition of celibacy or as sacred justification.

The Apostle Paul could make no absolute pronouncement on sexual abstinence (I Corinthians 7:25-26). Paul himself was a pharisaic scholar, middle-aged, and men in his position were usually married, as Jewish tradition equated marriage with duty. There is no reference in the Bible that Jesus was married or had sexual relationships with women.

Most pronouncements in the Gospels were made in light of the Second Coming of Christ (I Thessa-

> "Celibacy contributed to the independence of the Church and aided the Sovereign Pontiffs in building up that compact, well-organized hierarchy, which brought so many blessings upon European society in the ages of transition from barbarism to modern civilization . . . The reasons which have impelled the Church to impose celibacy upon the clergy are plain, simple, and cogent, and may be summed up thus: first, that they may serve God with less restraint, and with undivided heart; and second, that, being called to the altar, they may embrace the life of continence, which is holier than that of marriage."

> —By "J.C.," in his anonymously written response to the rise of anti-Catholic sentiments in *Why Should Priests Wed?* (1888)

lonians 4:17), which first-century Christians felt was imminent. In anticipation of Christ's return, the faithful should remain in the same state as when called to Christ—married or unmarried (I Corinthians 7:25-26). Even slaves, it said, should not seek to change their situation.

In the fourth century, Jerome (translator of the Vulgate, or common Latin version of the Bible) revised his translation of "wife" (in 383 A.D.) in I Corinthians 9:5 to "sister as a woman" (in 385 A.D.), which was interpreted as "Christian female servant," *not* a wife. That same year, Pope Siricius pronounced it a crime for priests to have sex with their wives after ordination.

Still, some historians indicate that many of the early popes were married or routinely had sex with women, as did many priests. Marriage for the clergy was not for-

mally forbidden until 1139, by Innocent II at the Second Lateran Council.

The question of celibacy cannot be separated from issues of economics and political power. Historically, there was a concern for the costs of supporting a priest's wife and children, along with the danger of "priest dynasties," which could lead to conflict with the pope or his appointed bishops and cause disputes over the ownership of church property. Those ignoring the ban were imprisoned, fined, tortured by starvation ("penitent fasting"), or beaten. Wives and children of priests could become slaves of the Church. Soldiers were often sent to persecute married priests and their families.

As was the case over four hundred years ago, the Catholic Church continues to be racked with dissent. Since 1965, an esti-

SUPPORT:
Now concerning the things whereof ye wrote unto me: It is good for a man not to touch a woman. Nevertheless, to avoid fornication, let every man have his own wife, and let every woman have her own husband.

—I Corinthians 7:1–2

A bishop then must be blameless, the husband of one wife, vigilant, sober, of good behaviour, given to hospitality, apt to teach.

—I Timothy 3:2

His disciples say unto him, If the case of the man be so with his wife, it is not good to marry. But he said unto them, All men cannot receive this saying, save they to whom it is given.

—Matthew 19:10–11

For this cause left I thee in Crete, that thou shouldest set in order the things that are wanting, and ordain elders in every city, as I had appointed thee: If any be blameless, the husband of one wife, having faithful children not accused of riot or unruly.

—Titus 1:5–6

"Celibacy is my shield from reality, my protection from people, the wall that bars me from concern . . ."

—Father James Kavanaugh in *A Modern Priest Looks at His Outdated Church* (1967)

"Why Should Priests Wed?"

Title page from "Why Should Priests Wed?" (1888)

SUPPORT:
Now the Spirit speaketh expressly, that in the latter times some shall depart from the faith, giving heed to seducing spirits, and doctrines of devils; Speaking lies in hypocrisy; having their conscience seared with a hot iron; Forbidding to marry, and commanding to abstain from meats, which God hath created to be received with thanksgiving of them which believe and know the truth. For every creature of God is good, and nothing to be refused, if it be received with thanksgiving: For it is sanctified by the word of God and prayer.

—I Timothy 4:1–5

mated 100,000 priests have left the Catholic clergy due to celibacy requirements, and seminary enrollment has dropped dramatically. Yet in his *Letter to All the Priests of the Church* (1979), John Paul II refers to "celibacy for the sake of the Kingdom of Heaven . . . He that is able to receive this, let him receive it" (Matthew 19:12).

Whether or not it is justified, current publicity surrounding sexual misconduct of priests is often used as an argument for optional celibacy. A worldwide policy of optional celibacy and ordination of women (both showing increased acceptance) could greatly increase the ranks of Catholic clergy and laity.

The Bible Tells Me So

Part Three

Behavior

Take heed that ye do not your alms before men, to be seen of them: otherwise ye shall have no reward of your Father which is in heaven.

—Matthew 6:1

44

"Marital intercourse, even with one's legitimate spouse, is forbidden and immoral, if the awakening of new life is prevented."

—Augustine, as quoted by Pius X (1930)

And there were also sodomites in the land: and they did according to all the abominations of the nations which the Lord cast out before the children of Israel.
—I Kings 14:24

Even as Sodom and Gomorrah, and the cities about them in like manner, giving themselves over to fornication, and going after strange flesh, are set forth for an example, suffering the vengeance of eternal fire.
—Jude 7

To Define and Punish the Crime of Sodomy

Sodomy has been defined as any form of non-procreative sex, even among married couples. Sodomy laws (originally involving the death penalty) have their origin in the story of Sodom and Gomorrah (in which the men of Sodom attempt a gang rape of men who are guests of Lot) and, by extension, the "sin of Onan," or the "spilling" of semen.

Secular sodomy laws are usually vague due to the fact that lawmakers often could not bring themselves to describe any sexual act. In some cases Scripture was incorporated word-for-word into law. The Massachusetts Bay Code of 1641 called for death for heresy, witchcraft, murder, treason, and "man lying with a man as with a woman," among other crimes. The New Haven Law of 1656 called for death for male-female anal intercourse, acts "against nature" between women, and "incitement to masturbation." Most sodomy laws, like the Washington, D.C., criminal code, forbade any type of sex other than basic male-female intercourse.

The definition of sodomy has changed over the centuries, alternately referred to as a "crime against nature," a "detestable and

As Sodom burns, Lot drinks wine prior to impregnating his daughters. Seventeenth-century engraving.

abominable vice," the "unspeakable vice of the Greeks," and "unnatural sin." Prosecution for sodomy is typically aimed at men. Generally speaking, women were thought incapable of sex without male participation.

Reverend Samuel Danforth, in a 1674 sermon, warned his congregation that failing to impose the death sentence for sodomy (among other crimes) would bring the wrath of God upon the New England colonies. Colonial lawmakers were selective in that they did not call for the biblically advocated death penalty on other sins such as adultery.

The sexual missionary position is so named because missionaries in remote regions, fearful that

The Bible Tells Me So

1: And there came two angels to Sodom at even; and Lot sat in the gate of Sodom: and Lot seeing them rose up to meet them; and he bowed himself with his face toward the ground;

2: And he said, Behold now, my lords, turn in, I pray you, into your servant's house, and tarry all night, and wash your feet, and ye shall rise up early, and go on your ways. And they said, Nay; but we will abide in the street all night.

3: And he pressed upon them greatly; and they turned in unto him, and entered into his house; and he made them a feast, and did bake unleavened bread, and they did eat.

4: But before they lay down, the men of the city, even the men of Sodom, compassed the house round, both old and young, all the people from every quarter:

5: And they called unto Lot, and said unto him, Where are the men which came in to thee this night? bring them out unto us, that we may know them.

6: And Lot went out at the door unto them, and shut the door after him,

7: And said, I pray you, brethren, do not so wickedly.

8: Behold now, I have two daughters which have not known man; let me, I pray you, bring them out unto you, and do ye to them as is good in your eyes: only unto these men do nothing; for therefore came they under the shadow of my roof.

9: And they said, Stand back. And they said again, This one fellow came in to sojourn, and he will needs be a judge: now will we deal worse with thee, than with them. And they pressed sore upon the man, even Lot, and came near to break the door.

10: But the men put forth their hand, and pulled Lot into the house to them, and shut to the door.

11: And they smote the men that were at the door of the house with blindness, both small and great: so that they wearied themselves to find the door.

12: And the men said unto Lot, Hast thou here any besides? son in law, and thy sons, and thy daughters, and whatsoever thou hast in the city, bring them out of this place:

13: For we will destroy this place, because the cry of them is waxen great before the face of the Lord; and the Lord hath sent us to destroy it.

15: And when the morning arose, then the angels hastened Lot, saying, Arise, take thy wife, and thy two daughters, which are here; lest thou be consumed in the iniquity of the city.

16: And while he lingered, the men laid hold upon his hand, and upon the hand of his wife, and upon the hand of his two daughters; the Lord being merciful unto him: . . . and set him without the city.

24: Then the Lord rained upon Sodom and upon Gomorrah brimstone and fire from the Lord out of heaven;

28: And [Abraham] looked toward Sodom and Gomorrah, and toward all the land of the plain, and beheld, and, lo, the smoke of the country went up as the smoke of a furnace.

—Genesis 19

Behavior

"It's real hard to tell yourself that people with disabilities shouldn't have sex because they can't in the one way that is legal here in Michigan."

—Verna Spayth, a disabled heterosexual who is unable to have traditional intercourse as a result of post-polio syndrome (1993)

natives would face eternal damnation for the practice of sodomy, taught them to engage instead in the "man on top" style.

The King James Version of the Bible was edited in the mid-1940s to alleviate confusion by occasionally substituting *sodomy* or *sodomite* with *homosexuality* or *homosexual,* words that didn't exist until the 1890s.

Enforcement of sodomy laws has been erratic at best. In Georgia, in 1988, a man was sentenced to five years in prison for having consensual oral sex with his wife. In the same year, a heterosexual man in North Carolina was sentenced to ten years in prison, also for oral sex. Most prosecution, however, has been directed at homosexuals. In the state of Maryland, the maximum penalty for sodomy is ten years; Virginia's law calls for twenty years.

In Atlanta, Georgia, in 1986, a man was arrested and convicted after a policeman found him having sex with another man in his own bedroom. The case, known as *Bowers* v. *Hardwick,* is often referred to in other cases involving sodomy law. In that case, the U.S. Supreme Court ruled that the constitutional right to privacy doesn't extend to *homosexual* sodomy.

Sodomy laws, once making sodomy a felony in all fifty states, have been repealed or ruled unconstitutional in twenty-six states. Several states have narrowed their laws to apply almost exclusively to gay men and lesbians. In 1993, a Virginia judge ruled that a woman would lose custody of her son because her relationship with another woman violated sodomy laws.

Surveys repeatedly show that a high percentage of married couples engage in sexual activity for purposes other than conception. Few fear prosecution.

"Vasectomy: Elective surgical procedure by which the body is altered to allow for sex without any chance of fertilization."

To Prevent Masturbation

In the story of Onan (Genesis 38:7–10), God sent Onan to impregnate his dead brother's wife. Onan instead committed coitus interruptus, spilling his "seed" and avoiding conception. God was not pleased, and slew him.

The curse of Onan has long been used to condemn any sexual act for any purpose other than procreation, particularly masturbation. Partner or no partner, the circumstances didn't matter to Scriptural authorities. And, strictly speaking, they still don't.

Orthodox Jewish laws sometimes required death for masturbation, prohibiting men from extending their hands below their waists, from touching their own genitals (married men were exempt, but only when urinating), and even looking at anyone else's genitalia. Tight pants and riding bareback were also frowned upon.

For almost three centuries, doctors of theology and medicine worked together to prevent the grave sin of onanism. And if the prospect of damnation wasn't frightening enough, Victorian-era doctors agreed "self-pollution" led to disturbances of the stomach and digestion, loss of appetite (or ravenous hunger), vomiting and

The facial effects of onanism. From "Boyhood's Perils and Manhood's Curse" (1858)

"The physical symptoms are weakness, pallor and backache and general debility. The effects on the brain and nervous system are more serious. They may dull the intellect, weaken the memory and the affections, produce listlessness, apathy, moroseness and morbid irritability, in short a general perversion of character . . ."

—Elwood Worcester, D.D., Ph.D., Samuel McComb, M.A., D.D., and Isador H. Coriat, M.D., in *Religion and Medicine: The Moral Control of Nervous Disorders* (1908)

And Er, Judah's firstborn, was wicked in the sight of the Lord; and the Lord slew him. And Judah said unto Onan, Go in unto thy brother's wife, and marry her, and raise up seed to thy brother. And Onan knew that the seed should not be his; and it came to pass, when he went in unto his brother's wife, that he spilled it on the ground, lest that he should give seed to his brother. And the thing which he did displeased the Lord: wherefore he slew him also.
—Genesis 38:7–10

Let not sin therefore reign in your mortal body, that ye should obey it in the lusts thereof. Neither yield ye your members as instruments of unrighteousness unto sin: but yield yourselves unto God, as those that are alive from the dead, and your members as instruments of righteousness unto God.
—Romans 6:12–13

And if any man's seed of copulation go out from him, then he shall wash all his flesh in water, and be unclean until the even. And every garment, and every skin whereon is the seed of copulation, shall be washed with water, and be unclean until the even.
—Leviticus 15:16–17

"onanism (ó-nan-ism): A term erroneously used to designate masturbation. Onan of the Bible really practiced coitus interruptus."

—Richard H. Hutchings, M.D., in *A Psychiatric Word Book* (1939)

"In the case of a man the hand that reaches below the belly-button should be chopped off.

—Ancient Jewish law

nausea, degeneration of the lungs and spinal cord, coughing and hoarseness, ear problems, paleness, thinness, softening or dehydration of the brain, epilepsy, and of course pimples, blindness, and insanity.

Clearly, youth were in danger. In this era, nutritionist and physician John Harvey Kellogg of Battle Creek, Michigan, believing that his "science" and good, wholesome food could steel young minds against unclean thoughts, developed his breakfast cereals and started a new industry in the process.

Periodically, the Vatican releases statements referring to masturbation as "an intrinsically and seriously disordered act," or a "mortal sin," as in Pope Paul VI's 1975 *Declaration on Some Questions in Sexual Ethics.* Pope John Paul II, in his 179-page encyclical, *Veritas Splendor* ("The Splendor of Truth"), released in 1993, condemns masturbation, among other

VICTORIAN-ERA MEDICAL TREATMENTS FOR MASTURBATION

Physical restraints

Lead bedsheets

Straitjacket pajamas

Erection alarms

Enemas

Infibulation (closing the foreskin with rings, clasps, or staples to prevent erection)

"Die Onanie-bandagen" (a metal device similar to a chastity belt)

Metal fitted rings containing spikes or razors

Wooden "eggs" inserted into the rectum

FOR EXTREMELY STUBBORN CASES:

Castration

Amputation of the penis

For females, a clitoridectomy

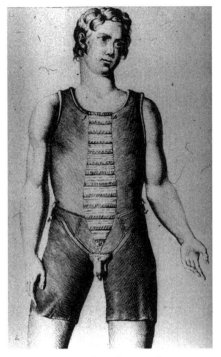

One of many devices invented to save children from onanism. Paris, nineteenth century.

The concern over masturbation has been for centuries directed exclusively at males. (In the act, "seed," once thought to contain tiny humans, is discarded rather than "sown." This explains why masturbation has been equated with murder, as has homosexuality, contraception, and sodomy.) Women were thought unable to experience sexual pleasure. Only fifty years ago, sexual desire by women was considered by many to be pathological.

The medical community no longer considers masturbation a major threat to public health (in spite of a potentially high case load: research indicates that 90 percent of males and 60 percent of females masturbate) unless it becomes a compulsion or is accompanied by excessive feelings of guilt or shame.

Nevertheless, the act still carries a stigma. In 1994, former U.S. Surgeon General Joycelyn Elders, responding to an audience question concerning masturbation as an alternative to unsafe sex in the age of AIDS, stated her belief that it is ". . . a part of human sexuality [which] . . . perhaps should be taught . . ." Her remarks, which her supporters felt were taken out of context, caused her to be promptly fired.

"The sex drive is the strongest human drive after hunger. . . . There must be an outlet. I am recommending self-gratification or mutual masturbation, whatever it takes to release the sexual energy. . . . I do not want to hear from clergymen telling me it's a sin. The sin is making people feel guilty about responding to this fundamental human drive."

—Columnist Ann Landers, in response to a letter discussing sex in the '90s (1993)

things, yet again. Any form of nonprocreative sex is against the will of God.

Modern technology has been employed to prevent the sin: Catholic University of the Sacred Heart in Rome (which is under the direction of Italian bishops), announced in 1993 the development of a "vibrating machine" that attaches to the testicles in order to gather sperm for medical purposes (excluding artificial insemination). This would allow donors to avoid the act of masturbation.

A pro-life message, emphasizing the "personhood" of the fetus

Thou shalt not kill.
—Exodus 20:13

Before I formed thee in the belly I knew thee; and before thou camest forth out of the womb I sanctified thee, and I ordained thee a prophet unto the nations.
—Jeremiah 1:5

And it came to pass, that, when Elisabeth heard the salutation of Mary, the babe leaped in her womb; and Elisabeth was filled with the Holy Ghost: And she spake out with a loud voice, and said, Blessed art thou among women, and blessed is the fruit of thy womb.
—Luke 1:41–42

To Oppose Abortion

Pregnancies were terminated through various means in the ancient world; the Bible does not specifically prohibit abortion.

Abortion's opponents use the Bible primarily to define the fetus as a person. By establishing "personhood," the case is made that abortion—killing a person, although unborn—is murder. Those with pro-choice views want the decision left to the woman concerned, arguing that such use of the Bible is simply desperate literal interpretation. They find no Scriptural proof to justify that a fetus is already a person, or "ensouled."

Jeremiah 1:5 and Luke 1:41–42 anticipate the arrival of a prophet with a particular mission from God. Exodus 21:22 describes the penalty for a man who causes a woman to miscarry as a result of assaulting her. The Hebrew words for the unborn are the same used as when speaking of young children or adolescents. The Greek word *baby* or *small child* is seen in Luke in reference to the unborn John the Baptist, the baby Jesus, and the children brought to Jesus to be blessed. Pregnant means "with child" (see Matthew 1:23). Many more verses are cited as proof that the fetus is a person.

The pro-choice side looks to the Bible to confirm the "personhood" of each *woman,* and her need for the freedom to make an individual decision in the light of her personal relationship with God, not with secular law. While opponents label pro-choicers as "pro-abortion," few pro-choicers encourage abortion as a casual form of birth control. They emphasize the need to prevent unsafe, illegal abortions, which result in the deaths of many women.

Issues of separation of church and state are also involved—if abortion were made unlawful in part based on biblical interpretation, then a woman electing to

"Abraham Lincoln recognized that we could not survive as a free land when some men could decide that others were not fit to be free and should therefore be slaves. Likewise, we cannot survive as a free nation when some men decide that others are not fit to live and should be abandoned to abortion or infanticide . . ."

—Ronald Reagan, *Abortion and the Conscience of the Nation* (1984)

The Bible Tells Me So

"[I can't believe that a Catholic] in good conscience [could vote for a political candidate who approves of abortion]."

" . . . [But I do not intend to tell] anyone to vote for or against anyone."

—Comments of Archbishop John J. O'Connor of New York as reported in *The New York Times* (June 25, 1984)

For thou hast possessed my reins: thou hast covered me in my mother's womb. I will praise thee; for I am fearfully and wonderfully made: marvellous are thy works; and that my soul knoweth right well. My substance was not hid from thee, when I was made in secret, and curiously wrought in the lowest parts of the earth.

—Psalm 139:13–15

If men strive, and hurt a woman with child, so that her fruit depart from her, and yet no mischief follow: he shall be surely punished, according as the woman's husband will lay upon him; and he shall pay as the judges determine.

—Exodus 21:22

have an abortion would be forced to abide by the religious beliefs of the majority.

Catholics, along with many Protestant and Jewish groups, have been politically active in fighting against any legalized form of abortion. In 1994, the Vatican opposed the objectives of the Third United Nations Conference on Population Growth, fearing the resulting document would promote abortion. To form an opposing coalition, the Vatican sent emissaries to countries governed under Islamic law, who shared the concerns of the Holy See.

Most people who oppose abortion on religious or Scriptural grounds do not actively participate in or encourage blocking access to clinics, intimidation, bombings, threats of blackmail, or coercion. They rely on their chosen political leaders to make abortion illegal. "Rescuers" in the vanguard of the militant anti-abortion movement encourage their followers to use these tactics with great religious conviction. Recently, the line has been crossed from extreme yet nonviolent protest to the maiming and killing of abortion providers.

On March 10, 1993, Michael F. Griffin, thirty-two, shot and killed abortion doctor David Gunn. Upon his arrest, Griffin claimed that the Bible would be his only defense. He was sentenced to life in prison, ironically spared the death penalty for his own execution of a "baby murderer." His lawyers claimed that anti-abortion literature, instruction, videos, and protest participation caused him temporary insanity.

On July 29, 1994, Paul Hill, forty, murdered abortion doctor John Britton and his escort in Pensacola, Florida. Hill, leader of the radical anti-abortion group Defensive Action, held a Master of Divinity degree and had served as a minister in the Presbyterian Church

If abortion is killing, act like it is murder."

—Randall Terry, Operation Rescue founder (1989)

Behavior

until he was ousted for his views on violence toward abortion providers. Prior to the murders, Hill had publicly stated that the killing of abortion providers would be analogous to killing Hitler, and that women who sought abortions were accessories to murder. The murder of abortionists, he claimed, could be biblically justified. He received the death sentence.

While mainstream leaders of anti-abortion religious and activist groups roundly denounce the murder of abortion providers, anti-abortion activists see themselves as continuing the great American tradition of civil disobedience, from abolitionists defying the Fugitive Slave Act to militant anti-war protestors decrying engagement in Vietnam. Evoking the image of the Holocaust, they see themselves in a "just war." They come from a wide variety of religious and activist backgrounds, from which many have been expelled. Federal investigators have as yet been unable to discover any organized

A seventeenth-century engraving of Mary and Elisabeth's encounter (Luke 1)

conspiracy among abortion opponents.

In 1994, the Freedom of Access Bill made it a federal offense to use force or threat of force to injure, intimidate, or block access to an abortion clinic, punishing violators with imprisonment and fines. Anti-abortion activists see the law as a form of religious persecution, limiting their freedom to practice their religious beliefs, turning their pro-life protests into a criminal activity.

A pro-choice image depicting a coat hanger to symbolize illegal and unsafe abortions

"[Christianity's] greatest outrage upon her was to forbid her to control the function of motherhood under any circumstances, thus limiting her life's work to bringing forth and rearing children."
"Woman's role has been that of an incubator and little more."
"Contraceptives or abortion—which shall it be?"

—Margaret Sanger, who favored making birth control available to women, *Woman and the New Race* (1920)

Children working at the furnace of a glass factory, 1914. Child labor is only recently considered a violation of human rights.

To Justify the Physical Punishment of Children

The decision to physically discipline one's children was, until recently, strictly a family matter and not openly discussed. Anyone looking for justification need only open the Bible to the Old Testament.

It states that all children, at birth, carry the burden of original sin as descendants of Adam and Eve, and have no relationship to God. They are ready and willing instruments of the Devil. (In the eighteenth century, religious leader Jonathan Edwards frequently referred to children as "little vipers.")

Accordingly, for most of the history of mankind, children were best seen and not heard, simply smaller versions of adults. Little effort was made to understand their inability to comprehend the adult world. Hard work and strong physical dis-

For every one that curseth his father or his mother shall be surely put to death . . .
                    —Leviticus 20:9

He that spareth his rod hateth his son: but he that loveth him chasteneth him betimes.
                    —Proverbs 13:24

Train up a child in the way he should go: and when he is old, he will not depart from it.
                    —Proverbs 22:6

Withhold not correction from the child: for if thou beatest him with the rod, he shall not die. Thou shalt beat him with the rod, and shalt deliver his soul from hell.
                    —Proverbs 23:13–14

Foolishness is bound in the heart of a child; but the rod of correction shall drive it far from him.
                    —Proverbs 22:15

Fathers, provoke not your children to anger, lest they be discouraged.
                    —Colossians 3:21

Lo, children are an heritage of the Lord: and the fruit of the womb is his reward.
                    —Psalm 127:3

54

> Then were there brought unto him little children, that he should put his hands on them, and pray: and the disciples rebuked them. But Jesus said, Suffer little children, and forbid them not, to come unto me: for of such is the kingdom of heaven. And he laid his hands on them, and departed thence.
>
> —Matthew 19:13–15

> It was meet that we should make merry, and be glad: for this thy brother was dead, and is alive again; and was lost, and is found.
>
> —Luke 15:32

cipline was thought to build character. For many guardians, one of their many roles was to "beat the Devil" out of wayward children, an idea probably stemming from the popular "biblical" quotation (actually a line from Samuel Butler's satiric rhyme of 1664), "Love is a boy by poets styled/Then spare the rod, and spoil the child."

Today, school discipline is a major problem, yet physical punishment by public school authorities is almost unheard of. Consequently, many Americans now advocate a return of corporal punishment as well as school prayer to return order and respect for authority. And studies show that those with a strong literal belief in the Bible tend to rely more on corporal punishment in dealing with their own children and favor it in schools.

The New Testament shows a different attitude concerning children, as evidenced in Jesus' requests to have children brought before him (Matthew 19:13–15)

"Mary Ellen." The subject of the first American case of child abuse to be prosecuted. (1874)

and in the parable of the prodigal son (Luke 15), in which an unruly youth benefits from the grace and forgiveness of his father.

One typical method of "teaching" children (1900)

> "The doctor took his son on his lap, and the child befouled him. Thereupon he [Martin Luther] said, 'How our Lord God has to put up with many a murmur and stink from us, worse than a mother must endure from her child!' "
>
> —Martin Luther (1532)

The Bible Tells Me So

A public buildings and grounds "cop" checks to make sure that hemlines on women's bathing suits are not more than six inches above the knee. (1922)

To Regulate Clothing and Hairstyles

The Bible contains several specific instructions concerning clothing and hairstyles, most of which differentiated the wardrobes of the chosen people from the fashions, and lifestyles, of the heathen majority.

Today, biblical regulations continue to be strictly observed by the members of some Jewish and Christian denominations and sects, for daily as well as Sabbath wear. The Amish provide an interesting case study in biblically inspired dress codes. They avoid clothing or accessories that draw attention to the wearer. Exposed buttons are seen as too ornamental and possibly frivolous. A watch, carried in the pocket, may be of nickel or silver, but never gold.

Behavior

Judge in yourselves: is it comely that a woman pray unto God uncovered? Doth not even nature itself teach you, that, if a man have long hair, it is a shame unto him? But if a woman have long hair, it is a glory to her: for her hair is given her for a covering.
—I Corinthians 11:13–15

Every man praying or prophesying, having his head covered, dishonoureth his head. But every woman that prayeth or prophesieth with her head uncovered dishonoureth her head: for that is even all one as if she were shaven. For if the woman be not covered, let her also be shorn: but if it be a shame for a woman to be shorn or shaven, let her be covered.
—I Corinthians 11:4–6

In like manner also, that women adorn themselves in modest apparel, with shamefacedness and sobriety; not with broided hair, or gold, or pearls, or costly array; But (which becometh women professing godliness) with good works.
—I Timothy 2:9–10

" . . . (I)t is a sin for women to put on male clothes, even a mortal sin . . . Those who are forced into it by their professions are to be pitied."

—From the book *Your Clothes* (1919), printed by a German Catholic priest under a pseudonym

And he said unto them in his doctrine, Beware of the scribes, which love to go in long clothing, and love salutations in the marketplaces.
—Mark 12:38

And they that use this world, as not abusing it: for the fashion of this world passeth away.
—I Corinthians 7:31

That he told her all his heart, and said unto her, There hath not come a razor upon mine head; for I have been a Nazarite unto God from my mother's womb: if I be shaven, then my strength will go from me, and I shall become weak, and be like any other man.
—Judges 16:17

Men shave only until marriage, growing a beard (but no mustache) thereafter. And at all times, the Amish woman wears a small cap known as a prayer cap, thus following the directions of I Corinthians 11:2–6.

In the past, dress codes have been forced on the general population because the alternatives posed a potential threat to the status quo. And the primary enforcement of these codes related to women.

The tradition of the veil for Catholic women can be traced back to passages in Corinthians. Some historians believe the injunction for a head covering stemmed from the fact that the more "exposed" or uncovered women of the day were often prostitutes. A woman was to avoid sending the wrong message to men, thereby "shaming" herself.

The Bible tells women to dress as plainly as men, for whom the temptation of flamboyance doesn't seem as great. Women were warned specifically to wear "modest apparel" and avoid braided hair, gold, pearls, and "costly array." John Wesley, in formulating the tenets of the Wesleyan Methodists, required of those seeking admission to his church that they avoid "doing what we know is not for the glory of God; as the putting on of gold or costly apparel; the taking of such diversions as cannot be used in the name of the Lord Jesus." Today, most of the devout would agree more with the "spirit" of this injunction as requiring them to avoid drawing attention to themselves. But this lesson was apparently lost on the flamboyant Christian televangelists of the '80s (both men and women), whose hairstyles, makeup, and wardrobes provided much unintended entertainment.

In Puritan New England, the Massachusetts General Court prohibited the purchase of any clothing with gold, silver, lace, or embroidery. Spending too much

"Should women ride [bicycles]? What should they wear? What are God's intentions concerning them? Should they ride on Sunday? These questions were asked with all seriousness. We had a symposium on these points in one of the daily papers. To me the answer to all these questions was simple—if woman could ride, it was evidently 'God's intention' that she be permitted to do so. As to what she should wear, she must decide what is best adapted to her comfort and convenience."

—Elizabeth Cady Stanton in *Eighty Years and More: Reminiscences 1815–1897*

The Bible Tells Me So

on personal adornment was a waste of money that could be used for other, more practical purposes. Clothing defined class and status. Poorer citizens were fined for dressing beyond their means. And the public morality had to be safeguarded: lax enforcement of clothing regulations was seen as part of the cause of the rise of illegitimate births and prostitution.

One of the most well-enforced biblical injunctions has dealt with "transvestism," or, specifically, whether women should be allowed to wear trousers (see Deuteronomy 22:5). In most Christian nations, civil laws have related to this, although it is ultimately more of an issue of women infringing on male turf. Some American homesteaders' wives, who usually worked as hard as men, kept a skirt within reach in order to cover their trousers, should a stranger or law officer happen by. Rosa Bonheur, a nineteenth-century French artist, had to renew a police permit every six months in order to wear pants

Adam and Eve, the inspiration for the Adamites, a number of heretical sects who rejected clothing and marriage in order to attain the primitive innocence of the first couple. Appearing at various times from the second century to the eighteenth, they were thought to have inspired some of the figures in the paintings of Hieronymus Bosch, allegedly a member of the sect himself. Often, Adamites were rounded up and forcibly clothed or slaughtered. Seventeenth-century engraving.

while doing research for her paintings in stockyards and livestock markets. American Amelia Jenks Bloomer (1818–1894) devised a political fashion statement and caused an uproar. "Bloomers"

"There will be fashion in heaven as on earth, but it will be a different kind of fashion. It will decide the color of the dress; and the population of that country, by a beautiful law, will wear white."

—The Reverend T. DeWitt Talmage, D.D., *Social Dynamite; or the Wickedness of Modern Society* (1890)

They shall not make baldness upon their head, neither shall they shave off the corner of their beard, nor make any cuttings in their flesh.

—Leviticus 21:5

The woman shall not wear that which pertaineth unto a man, neither shall a man put on a woman's garment: for all that do so are abomination unto the Lord thy God.

—Deuteronomy 22:5

Strength and honour are her clothing; and she shall rejoice in time to come.

—Proverbs 31:25

And why take ye thought for raiment? Consider the lilies of the field, how they grow; they toil not, neither do they spin: and yet I say unto you that even Solomon in all his glory was not arrayed like one of these.

—Matthew 6:28–29

"It often surprises me that professing Christians, with this blessed book in hand, do not perceive their duty with more clearness . . . The truth is that FASHION is a *tyrant,* and rules its votaries with a rod of iron. Over the world her supremacy is entire, and over the Church it is but little less."

—From a story in *Caroline Jones; or, Outward and Inward Adorning* (1860)

Behavior

58

"... the goddess of fashion has set up her throne in this country ... The old and new testament of her bible are *Madame Demorest's Magazine* and *Harper's Bazar* [sic] ... This goddess of fashion has become a rival of the Lord of heaven and earth, and it is high time that we come to count the victims of fashion ..."

—The Reverend T. DeWitt Talmage, D.D., *Social Dynamite; or the Wickedness of Modern Society* (1890)

THE LADY OF FASHION.   THE SENSIBLE WOMAN.

"The Lady of Fashion" and "The Sensible Woman" (1854)

"The Bloomer Costume" (1851)

allowed women to wear trousers, of sorts, under their dresses. Women who sported this style (including Susan B. Anthony and Elizabeth Cady Stanton) were crusading for dress reform as well as the right for women to vote.

In the twentieth century, fashion continued to reflect controversial issues facing a Christian society—the emancipation of women, the blurring of gender roles, a disrespect for the older generation, and the state of public morality.

Many young men took the brunt of criticism in the 1960s. At the time of the British Invasion (three centuries after Calvinists chased the Quakers down the streets to cut their hair), American teenage boys wanted a "Beatle cut." From many a pulpit, young men were warned against yet another crime of transvestism: "Doth not even nature itself teach you, that, if a man have long hair, it is a shame unto him?" (I Corinthians 11:14). Bangs were for girls.

Such a literal interpretation confused many an adolescent boy when looking at a picture of Jesus.

Part Four

Guilt, Crime, and Punishment

But I say unto you, That ye resist not evil: but whosoever shall smite thee on thy right cheek, turn to him the other also.

—Matthew 5:39

A hysterical woman is healed by a priest who drives out a demon (sixteenth century). Even into the twentieth century, mental illness was often attributed to demonic possession.

> And it was so, that, after they had carried it about, the hand of the Lord was against the city with a very great destruction: and he smote the men of the city, both small and great, and they had emerods [tumors] in their secret parts.
> —I Samuel 5:9

> The leprosy therefore of Naaman shall cleave unto thee, and unto thy seed for ever. And he went out from his presence a leper as white as snow.
> —II Kings 5:27

> And it came to pass that night, that the angel of the Lord went out, and smote in the camp of the Assyrians an hundred fourscore and five thousand: and when they arose early in the morning, behold, they were all dead corpses.
> —II Kings 19:35

To Assign Guilt for Disease

The discovery of Acquired Immune Deficiency Syndrome (AIDS) in the early 1980s brought many religious leaders and television evangelists to consider the "gay plague" an appropriate consequence of offending God.

Types of behavior and groups of people condemned in the Bible have frequently incurred God's wrath in the form of disease. Biblical sinners were often punished with "leprosy" (not the same disease as it is known today), a horrible skin disorder that left its sufferers deformed—an obvious sign of the consequence of sin. Jesus often healed those suffering from disease or congenital afflictions (John 9).

Just as Israel was punished with a plague, guilt for the Black Plague of the fourteenth century was shared between witches, who angered God, and the already biblically condemned Jews, who were accused of poisoning Christian water supplies. The English cholera epidemic of 1832 was said to be God's punishment for alcohol consumption (coinciding

She may be..
a bag of
TROUBLE
SYPHILIS · GONORRHEA

The "lady in red," carrier of venereal disease. U.S. government poster intended to warn the troops (circa 1940)

And Azariah the chief priest, and all the priests, looked upon him, and, behold, he was leprous in his forehead, and they thrust him out from thence; yea, himself hasted also to go out, because the Lord had smitten him. And Uzziah the king was a leper unto the day of his death, and dwelt in a several house, being a leper; for he was cut off from the house of the Lord: and Jotham his son was over the king's house, judging the people of the land.

—II Chronicles 26:20–21

"Cotton Mather called syphilis a punishment 'which the Just Judgment of God has reserved for our Late Ages.' Recalling this and other nonsense uttered about syphilis from the end of the fifteenth to the early twentieth centuries, one should hardly be surprised that many want to view AIDS . . . as, plague-like, a moral judgment on society."

—Susan Sontag, *AIDS and Its Metaphors* (1989)

with the early days of the anti-alcohol temperance movement). In the New World (about 1616) a tribe of Native Americans, probably in retaliation for a slave raid by whites, captured and killed most of the survivors of a wrecked French ship. One of their captives told them that "God was angry . . . and would destroy them, and give their country to another people, that should not live as beasts as

62

SILENCE = DEATH

A slogan used in AIDS awareness, which also holds true for many diseases (such as breast cancer and addictions) that were never talked about until fairly recently.

> But the Spirit of the Lord departed from Saul, and an evil spirit from the Lord troubled him. And Saul's servants said unto him, Behold now, an evil spirit from God troubleth thee. Let our lord now command thy servants which are before thee, to seek out a man, who is a cunning player on an harp: and it shall come to pass, when the evil spirit from God is upon thee, that he shall play with his hand, and thou shalt be well.
> —I Samuel 16:14–16

> For my loins are filled with a loathsome disease: and there is no soundness in my flesh. I am feeble and sore broken: I have roared by reason of the disquietness of my heart. Lord, all my desire is before thee; and my groaning is not hid from thee.
> —Psalm 38:7–9

they did, but should be clothed." Within a year, an epidemic (probably typhus or another flea- or louse-borne disease) decimated the tribes.

"God's punishment" of Native Americans was more likely diseases brought by foreign invaders.

Venereal disease of the late 1800s was caused by prostitutes (their clients were apparently exempt from blame). Syphilis reached epidemic proportions during the 1930s, illicit sex providing both a means of transmission and the necessary proof of divine punishment. To protect the innocent, parents advised covering toilet seats. They still do.

More recently, AIDS brought reaction from religious leaders as well as hate groups who interpret the Bible for their own means. Television evangelist Jerry Falwell stated that "AIDS is God's judgment on a society that does not live by His rules." Neo-Nazi leader Harold Covington wrote, "those four little letters . . . are God's greatest gift to our cause since the Fuhrer Adolph Hitler himself: AIDS!"

A terrified public turned to the government for guidance. According to Randy Shilts's book documenting the AIDS crisis, *And the Band Played On,* members of the Reagan administration met with

A seventeenth-century woodcut showing a plague doctor in protective clothing. Three centuries later, AIDS patients faced medical professionals who also took drastic precautions.

Jerry Falwell's Moral Majority before consulting health department officials in determining how to deal with America's already-tainted blood supply. Since AIDS seemed to affect only homosexual men, the administration apparently saw no reason to assume any danger of an epidemic; therefore, little energy or funding was allocated to fight the disease.

The Bible Tells Me So

Government-supported "safe sex" guidelines, the content of which was overseen by religious leaders as well as influential politicians, were vague, mentioning "bodily fluids" rather than blood and semen, further confusing the populace. The use of condoms, the only reasonably reliable means for sexually active people to avoid contracting the disease, is still prohibited by the Catholic Church. In reference to condom distribution in prison, Cardinal John O'Connor asked whether New York City mayor Ed Koch "can't prevent criminal action even in your own jail cells . . . ?" He also wrote, "I have yet to see any reliable evidence that either condoms or clean needles will [control the spread of] AIDS."

After more than a decade, AIDS is still considered an affliction of the "guilty." One "ex-gay" ministry, Love In Action, went so far as to videotape a dying AIDS patient as he confessed his sin and admitted guilt for his fate. Yet, although early reaction to AIDS from the religious community seemed more concerned with placing blame and saving souls rather than saving lives, many churches now realize their responsibility for nonjudgmental caring and outreach.

Meanwhile, cancer continues to claim millions of lives, often as a result of behaviors such as smoking, inactivity, and eating foods high in fat. In spite of the fact that lifestyle is an obvious precursor to diseases other than AIDS, the victims of these diseases are rarely blamed from a biblical standpoint. Yet disease still holds religious connotations, as evidenced by modern "sin taxes" levied on alcohol and tobacco.

"Caricatures anti-cholérique." Prostitutes were often accused of carrying cholera.

Guilt, Crime, and Punishment

63

And the anger of the Lord was kindled against them; and he departed. And the cloud departed from off the tabernacle; and, behold, Miriam became leprous, white as snow: and Aaron looked upon Miriam, and, behold, she was leprous.
—Numbers 12:9–10

And as Jesus passed by, he saw a man which was blind from his birth. And his disciples asked him, saying, Master, who did sin, this man, or his parents, that he was born blind? Jesus answered, Neither hath this man sinned, nor his parents: but that the works of God should be made manifest in him.
—John 9:1–3

". . . For Christian thinkers from Dante to Luther and the Puritans, the body's discomfort was a sign of the soul's distemper . . . bodily health depended on overcoming sin."
—Jackson Lears, professor of history, Rutgers University

Sign at a Greyhound bus station, Rome, Georgia (1943)

> And Noah began to be an husbandman, and he planted a vineyard: And he drank of the wine, and was drunken; and he was uncovered within his tent. And Ham, the father of Canaan, saw the nakedness of his father, and told his two brethren without. And Shem and Japheth took a garment, and laid it upon both their shoulders, and went backward, and covered the nakedness of their father; and their faces were backward, and they saw not their father's nakedness. And Noah awoke from his wine, and knew what his younger son had done unto him. And he said, Cursed be Canaan; a servant of servants shall he be unto his brethren. And he said, Blessed be the Lord God of Shem; and Canaan shall be his servant. God shall enlarge Japheth, and he shall dwell in the tents of Shem; and Canaan shall be his servant.
>
> —Genesis 9:20–27

To Argue the Inferiority of Black Peoples

People of African descent have suffered slavery, persecution, and discrimination in Christian nations for centuries. Some of those in power have justified their subjugation of blacks by referring to what has become known as the sin of Ham or the curse of Canaan.

In Genesis 9, Noah is sleeping naked, in a drunken stupor. His son, Ham, comes upon him, and rather than covering him runs and tells his brothers. Shem and Japheth, the "good" sons, promptly cover their father's nakedness. In reaction to Ham's sinful act of looking upon the "nakedness of the father," Noah puts a curse on his grandson, Ham's son, Canaan: "Cursed be Canaan, slave of slaves shall he be to his brothers."

The curse gradually came to be interpreted to mean that Ham was literally turned black, and that his descendants would be similarly cursed, a color-coding that would in turn label them as the subservient race.

When or how this interpretation first gained widespread acceptance is subject to debate. The fact that it came to be taken for granted is best seen in the many cases where political and religious leaders felt the need to refute it:

Republican Hinton Rowan Helper (1860) on slave holders: "[they] bandy among themselves, in traditionary order, certain garbled passages of Scripture, such, for

ON BEING BROUGHT FROM AFRICA TO AMERICA, 1768.

'Twas mercy brought me from my Pagan land,
Taught my benighted soul to understand
That there's a God, that there's a Saviour too:
Once I redemption neither sought nor knew.
Some view our sable race with scornful eye,
"Their colour is a diabolic die."
Remember, Christians, Negros, black as Cain,
May be refin'd, and join th'angelic train.

—Phillis Wheatley (1753–1784), "Negro Servant to Mr. John Wheatley, of Boston, in New England," from *Poems on Various Subjects, Religious and Moral* (1773)

And if thou say in thine heart, Wherefore come these things upon me? For the greatness of thine iniquity are thy skirts discovered, and thy heels made bare. Can the Ethiopian change his skin, or the leopard his spots? then may ye also do good, that are accustomed to do evil. Therefore will I scatter them as the stubble that passeth away by the wind of the wilderness. This is thy lot, the portion of thy measures from me, saith the Lord; because thou hast forgotten me, and trusted in falsehood.

—Jeremiah 13:22–25

instance, as that concerning poor old besotted Noah's intemperate curse of Ham, which . . . they regard, or pretend to regard, as investing them with full and perfect license to practise [slavery]."

Meanwhile, Reverend Gilbert Haven: "One text alone, in the whole Bible, can they bring to the support of African slavery. Every other reference to it is human, not specific—the slavery of Man, not Ham."

A century later, Reverend Martin Luther King, Jr.: "The greatest blasphemy of the whole ugly process was that the white man ended up making God his partner in the exploitation of the Negro."

The long-forgotten source of this interpretation in Christian nations can be traced to a "legend" or folk interpretation of the story collected by scholars of the Talmud. Historians assign a variety of dates for the legend, from the fifth to tenth centuries. Arabs, familiar with the legend, also believed that race branded black people as slaves.

In modern refutations, biblical scholars have noted that the ancient Hebrew word *ham* does not necessarily translate as "burnt" or "black," which had become a popular way of explaining the story. Even today, a survey of many readily available Bible references, while generally debunking the interpretation, reveals little consensus on how to interpret it. This is further complicated with the conclusions of some Afrocentrists that while not "cursed," Ham—along with many other characters of the Old Testament—was black.

"Nothing whatever in the Scriptures indicates that this curse consisted in a change of the color of the persons involved, though it is known that the Canaanites were dark-skinned. All that is disclosed is that Canaanites . . . shall be a servile race, never dominant for any length of time, always subjugated in the end."

—Carl F. H. Henry (consulting editor), *The Biblical Expositor: The Living Theme of The Great Book with General and Introductory Essays and Exposition for Each Book of the Bible* (1960, 1973)

In the American Jim Crow era, advertisements frequently featured insulting images of blacks.

Jeremiah 13:22-25 has also been interpreted in a racist manner, inspiring the title for Reverend Thomas Dixon's *The Leopard's Spots* of 1902. Fifty years earlier, Reverend Haven had a different interpretation, asking "'Can the Ethiopian change his skin?'—not because it is desirable, but because it is impossible . . ."

At various times, science has partnered with theology in perpetuating ideas of racial superiority of whites. Nonwhites were actually considered another species. Eve, they believed, was indeed the mother of all mankind—of the true, superior humans: whites.

A group of important nineteenth-century figures in the new science of physical anthropology promoted this polygenesist concept of race—different "humans" came from different sources. While the consensus was that all white men were created equal, could it be, with the major differences between the races, that all humans were the product of the same biblical creation? Their intent was not necessarily to promote slavery. Their major critics were found in the camp of the biblical literalists, who saw such theories as contradicting the Genesis story.

In 1924, *Eugenics in Relation to the New Family and the Law on Racial Integrity (including a paper read before the American Public Health Association)* was issued by the Bureau of Vital Statistics, State Board of Health, Richmond, Virginia, for distribution to state public health workers. It contains the "scientific" arguments for racial purity and the law against miscegenation: "The mental and moral characteristics of a black man cannot even under the best environments . . . become the same as those of a white man . . . indubitable scientific fact . . . culturally destructive [Negro] characters are hereditary, carried in the germ plasm . . ." The publication's author, Virginia State Registrar of Vital Statistics, W. A. Plecker, emphasized that our forefathers "came, not as did the Spanish and Portuguese adventurers of the southern continent, without their women, . . . but they came bring-

"The European or Caucasian is the most noble of the five races of men. It excels all others in learning and the arts, and includes the most powerful nations of ancient and modern times. The most valuable institutions of society, and the most important and useful inventions have originated with the people of this race."

—From a geography school textbook, *A System of Modern Geography* (1847)

> "We assert that in all countries and at all times there must be a class of hewers of wood and drawers of water who must always of necessity be the substratum of society. We affirm that it is best for all that this class should be formed of a race upon whom God himself has placed a mark of physical and mental inferiority."
>
> —From an article in the *Southern Literary Messenger* (1858)

ing their families, the Bible, and high ideals of religious and civic freedom." According to this official state document against mixed-race marriage, slavery had been a bad institution because it brought the "pollution of Negro blood" into America.

Today, it's almost impossible to comprehend the Bible, much less science, being used in this manner. Yet recently—even in the 1950s and 1960s—desegregation, or "race mixing," was often considered to be un-Christian. The "curse" lingered on. Now some physical and social scientists have taken up this lead, particularly on the issue of supposed inferior black intelligence. The debate over the inherent mental inferiority of blacks was reignited upon publication of *The Bell Curve* in 1994.

In the United States, racism was a legalized institution. Jim Crow laws required the separation of the races in public places. There were whites-only and colored-only water fountains, rest rooms, Laundromats, motels, restaurants, and schools. This wasn't just a Southern phenomenon—African-Americans enjoyed few legal protections anywhere. Racism permeated popular American culture, from plays and motion pictures to television and advertising.

In a self-described "Christian" nation, acknowledging the rights and humanity of nonwhites became, for many, an unprecedented, un-Christian concept. As W. A. Plecker summarized in his 1924 speech on racial purity and white superiority, "Let us turn a deaf ear to those who would interpret Christian brotherhood to mean racial equality."

Phyllis Wheatley (1753–1784), slave and poet

> In the antebellum South, "blacks were considered less than human . . . the Christian right's position was we were the cursed descendants of Ham. That was the Christian Coalition of that time."
>
> —Jesse L. Jackson, while speaking about the "manipulative use of Christianity" by the Christian Coalition of today (1994)

To Justify Discrimination, Intolerance, and Violence Toward Homosexuals

Emperor Caesar Flavius Anicius Justinianus (Justinian I, 483–565) was convinced that the earthquakes, famine, and pestilence his empire had suffered were the consequence of God's wrath upon homosexuals. Section 4.18 of the Justinian Code, dated November 21, 533, specifies death for "those who dare to indulge their unspeakable lust with males," as well as for heterosexual adulterers.

Medieval religious authorities prescribed burning at the stake (the term *faggot* originally referred to a piece of kindling such as that used to light the fire under a criminal sentenced to burn), strangulation, and hanging for homosexuals. Not as punishment, but rather as cure, since death prevented further sin by providing release from the earthly temptations of the flesh—an interesting, albeit severe, version of the modern Christian saying, "Hate the sin, love the sinner."

Lesbians were less prone to execution. Since there was no man involved, what they did didn't constitute "sex"; they were usually accused of witchcraft instead.

Following European witch

The pink triangle, used to identify homosexuals in Nazi Germany. The letter *B* probably indicated a prisoner of Belgian origin (circa 1938–45). Liberating Allies typically turned freed homosexuals back over to German authorities for reimprisonment.

mania, homosexuals, like witches, made the transition from heretic to simple felon; they were burned, beheaded, garroted, and drowned. In America, the words of the Bible were directly incorporated into anti-homosexual statutes in five of the original thirteen colonies, and expanded to include lesbianism in Connecticut.

The death penalty for homosexuality was eventually repealed in all of the original colonies, the last being South Carolina (1873). Many jurisdictions now rely instead on sodomy laws to punish homosexuals.

Church, state, and medical authorities for most of this century

And God blessed them, and God said unto them, Be fruitful, and multiply, and replenish the earth, and subdue it: and have dominion over the fish of the sea, and over the fowl of the air, and over every living thing that moveth upon the earth.
—Genesis 1:28

Therefore shall a man leave his father and his mother, and shall cleave unto his wife: and they shall be one flesh.
—Genesis 2:24

agreed from research into homo-sexuality that homosexuals were depraved, criminal, and mentally ill; of course, virtually all test subjects were selected from prisons and mental wards. In the 1950s Evelyn Hooker contradicted this view by studying subjects taken from the general populace. Yet, lobotomy, castration, and shock therapy were used both privately and by the U.S. government as a "cure" for homosexuality, even though, then as now, nothing could be shown to change sexual orientation.

"Thank God for AIDS"

"AIDS Kills Fags Dead"

"My Bible Says Homosexuality Is Wrong"

"God Hates Fags"

"God Said Kill Fags"

"Fear God Not Fags"

"Fag God=Rectum (Phil. 3:19)"

"Fags Doom Nations"

"Family Rights Forever, 'Gay' Rights Never!"

"Sodomites Burn In Hell"

—A sample of signs carried at "family values" rallies and anti-gay protests

The American Psychiatric Association stopped classifying homosexuality as a disease in 1973. The Christian establishment, however, remains firm in its position. The term *homosexual* was fitted into a revised translation of the Bible in the 1940s.

In the 1970s, religious entertainer Anita Bryant led a successful movement to prevent laws prohibiting anti-gay discrimination. "Since homosexuals cannot reproduce," she said, "they must freshen their ranks with our children . . ." Gay groups responded, "We *are* your children."

Concentration camps were rumored to be under construction to contain homosexuals. The rumors reappeared when Jesse Helms, Pat Robertson, and others representing the religious right reacted to the AIDS crisis in the early 1980s. A handful of religious leaders and conservative government officials called for quarantine camps to "protect the innocent." Moral Majority spokesman Reverend Greg Dixon remarked in 1983: "If homosexuals are not stopped, they will in time infect the entire nation, and America will be destroyed." And in March 1984, television evangelist Jerry Falwell declared homosexuals ". . . brute beasts . . . part of a vile and satanic system [that] will be utterly anni-

Thou shalt not lie with mankind, as with womankind: it is abomination.

—Leviticus 18:22

Know ye not that the unrighteous shall not inherit the kingdom of God? Be not deceived: neither fornicators, nor idolaters, nor adulterers, nor effeminate, nor abusers of themselves with mankind. Nor thieves, nor covetous, nor drunkards, nor revilers, or extortioners, shall inherit the kingdom of God.

—I Corinthians 6:9–10

There shall be no whore of the daughters of Israel, nor a sodomite of the sons of Israel. Thou shalt not bring the hire of a whore, or the price of a dog, into the house of the Lord thy God for any vow: for even both these are abomination unto the Lord thy God.

—Deuteronomy 23:17–18

70

Wherefore God also gave them up to uncleanness through the lusts of their own hearts, to dishonor their own bodies between themselves: . . . For this cause God gave them up unto vile affections: for even their women did change the natural use into that which is against nature: And likewise also the men, leaving the natural use of the woman, burned in their lust one toward another; men with men working that which is unseemly, and receiving in themselves that recompence of their error which was meet.

—Romans 1:24, 26–27

If a man also lie with mankind, as he lieth with a woman, both of them have committed an abomination: they shall surely be put to death; their blood shall be upon them.

—Leviticus 20:13

"Homosexuality makes God vomit."

—Reverend Jay Grimstead, director, Coalition on Revival (in *The Advocate,* October 20, 1992)

Homosexuals were often "purified" by burning, as this would release them from temptations of the flesh. Today, some demand the death penalty for homosexuality, still using justification found in the Bible.

hilated, and there will be a celebration in heaven."

Angered by President-elect Bill Clinton's pro-gay stance, fundamentalists demanded that evangelist Billy Graham break his long tradition of leading the nation in the inaugural prayer.

Scientific evidence strongly suggests that homosexuality is a biologically determined trait, not a "lifestyle" choice, news not well received by the religious right. According to Pat Robertson's Christian Broadcasting Network, "A great lie has sprung up about the gay life . . . the lie says: 'gays can-

not help the way they are. They're born that way. Homosexuals can't change.' This is simply not true." Several "ex-gay" ministries have sprung up, each claiming the ability to produce a "cure" for homosexuality through religious conversion and, among other means, teaching gay men to play football and work on cars. Exodus International, one of the first and largest, was abandoned after ten years by founders Michael Bussee and Gary Cooper after they realized themselves unable to alter their own sexual orientation.

"Homosexuality makes God

vomit," according to Jay Grimstead, director of the Coalition on Revival, a reconstructionist group that seeks to impose Old Testament laws in the place of the American legal system. ". . . We do believe that homosexuals and abortionists are committing murder, but most of us do not support the death penalty for them. This means that we are not being entirely consistent with the Bible, I know, but most of us are not promoting that at this time."

The Ku Klux Klan, long known for hatred and intimidation of Jews, blacks, Catholics, and immigrants, also advocates death for homosexuals, ostensibly for many of the same biblical reasons.

On Capitol Hill, during debate over a gay rights ordinance, one Senator cited the story of Lot and Sodom (Genesis 19). He failed to mention that Lot offered his two daughters to the angry mob and that he subsequently impregnated them himself (Genesis 19:8; 30–38).

Biblical Abominations:

Adultery

Certain animals

Eating a sacrificial offering

Eating pork

Egyptians eating bread with Hebrews

Fornication

Dishonest scales

Idol worship

Incense

Killing innocents

Lawbreakers

Lying

Lust and prostitution

Man (collectively)

Man lying with man

Marrying the daughter of a foreign god

Obstinance or disobedience

Oppression of the poor, robbery, usury

Pride

Unclean or unsanitary food

Sacrificial offerings from the wicked

Spreading discord

". . . that which is highly esteemed among men . . ."

Race-mixing

"French Fagot-vender." The derogatory term *faggot* probably evolved from the word used to describe kindling wood for starting a fire such as that used to execute criminals.

Guilt, Crime, and Punishment

"The Simpering Man," a stereotypically effeminate man, presumably homosexual. Illustration from the book *Social Dynamite: or, the Wickedness of Modern Society* (1890).

In 1992 the state of Colorado passed Amendment 2, prohibiting the enforcement of any local "special rights" ordinances for homosexuals. During the campaign, many invoked Leviticus 18:22 (calling homosexuality "an abomination") in favor of the amendment. Few read the Bible in terms of how it could affect the Colorado University football team; Deuteronomy 14:8 contains an injunction against the old pigskin (football): "and the swine . . . ye shall not . . . touch their dead carcass."

In 1992, several localities in Oregon passed Measure 9, which commands state, regional, and local governments to "[set] a standard for Oregon's youth that recognizes that homosexuality [is] . . . abnormal, wrong, unnatural, and perverse . . ."

The Catholic Church threw its support behind anti-gay legislation.

"[W]ithout antidiscrimination laws that specifically include sexual orientation, lesbians and gays can be kicked out of their apartments, denied service in restaurants and hotels, and fired from their jobs . . ."

—Heather Rhoads in *The Progressive,* March 1993

"The Bible advocates discrimination against, intolerance of, and the death penalty for homosexuals."

—Reverend Pete Peters (as quoted in *The "Christian" Agenda Revealed,* a pamphlet produced by Gran Fury, 1993)

In November 1992, the Vatican released a statement declaring that anti-discrimination legislation could "encourage a person with a homosexual orientation to declare his homosexuality or even to seek a partner." Yet a previous Vatican statement had stated that gays "do not choose their homosexual orientation; for most of them it is an ordeal . . . all manner of unjust discrimination should be avoided with respect to them."

The pope's subsequent statements reaffirm the Church's belief that homosexuality is nonetheless sinful.

The FBI found that "religious bias" accounted for 18 percent of anti-gay hate crimes committed in 1993.

And it came to pass, when he had made an end of speaking unto Saul, that the soul of Jonathan was knit with the soul of David, and Jonathan loved him as his own soul . . . Then Jonathan and David made a covenant, because he loved him as his own soul. And Jonathan stripped himself of the robe that was upon him, and gave it to David, and his garments, even to his sword, and to his bow, and to his girdle.

—I Samuel 18:1, 3–4

In spite of accusations that gays want to destroy the family unit, many same-sex couples maintain committed, monogamous relationships lasting longer than many marriages. Same-sex marriage is illegal in the United States, although several challenges to the law are currently in progress.

To Provide Spiritual Strength and Acceptance to Homosexuals

David and Jonathan were two men dedicated to each other with a commitment "passing the love of women." Ruth was similarly attached to Naomi, her statement of commitment so powerful, so loving,

it became the core of most modern Christian wedding ceremonies.

Gay people can see themselves in the Bible, but not necessarily in the fire and brimstone of Sodom and Gomorrah.

The story of Sodom and Gomorrah has often been called upon to justify intolerance of gays. Yet many believe the story deals not with homosexuality but with gang

"Jesus is going to do to Jerry [Falwell] and the others just what he did with the money-changers . . . This was a house of prayer, and he's turned it into a den of thieves . . . His program is just an infomercial for hate."

—Mel White, former ghostwriter for Jerry Falwell, Pat Robertson, and a number of other fundamentalist leaders, who has finally come to accept his own "God-given" homosexuality after denying it for years

I am distressed for thee, my brother Jonathan: very pleasant hast thou been unto me: thy love to me was wonderful, passing the love of women.

—II Samuel 1:26

And Ruth said [to Naomi], Intreat me not to leave thee, or to return from following after thee: for whither thou goest, I will go; and where thou lodgest, I will lodge: thy people shall be my people, and thy God my God: Where thou diest, will I die, and there will I be buried: the Lord do so to me, and more also, if ought but death part thee and me.

—Ruth 1:16–17

There is neither Jew nor Greek, there is neither bond nor free, there is neither male nor female: for ye are all one in Christ Jesus.

—Galatians 3:28

rape, used as a violent form of control dominance, or punishment (such as that which occurs during wartime and in prison).

For centuries, homosexuals have been victims of what many Christians now believe to be biblical misinterpretation. Leviticus 18:22 is an example of the influence of pagan customs during biblical times, some of which involved bestiality and animal sacrifice; one involved a "ministry" consisting entirely of sex as a form of worship. (Similar heterosexual "Christian" groups exist today, such as the Children of God, with twelve thousand members in seventy countries.)

I Corinthians 6:9–10 warns that "fornicators, nor idolaters, nor adulterers, nor effeminate, nor abusers of themselves with mankind [both the latter merged and changed to "homosexuals" in some post-1940 versions of the Bible], nor thieves, nor covetous, nor drunkards . . . will . . . inherit the Kingdom of God." Here, the condemned behaviors are destructive, involving not love but the use of people. Homosexuality per se is, again, not mentioned.

The story of the eunuch in Acts 8:27 shows that the church is open even to those incapable of producing children or having "normal" sexual activity. Matthew 8:5,

in which Jesus healed the centurion's "servant" (the original Greek reads "beloved boy"), suggests a homosexual relationship, according to John J. McNeil, a Manhattan psychotherapist who spent forty years as a Jesuit priest.

In 1993, the first draft of an official church document, "The Church and Human Sexuality: A Lutheran Perspective," asks whether ". . . the church should be loving and accepting of persons who are homosexual . . . but clearly oppose their being sexually active" and states that "To tell them they will never be able to live out who they are as sexual beings is cruel, not loving."

In fact, the Bible includes no approval of sexual activity, even among married (presumably heterosexual) couples, unless procreation is the main goal. Adultery warranted a death sentence. Period. Jesus frequently condemned those whose behavior He

"Every day, the church's position against gays and lesbians looks more like the positions it took against Copernicus and Galileo."

—Brian McNeill, president, Dignity Twin Cities Chapter

"It is fair to expect that if biblical fundamentalists are going to follow the dictates of *Leviticus* to the literal letter, they will show equal nicety in adhering to the rest of the "original" (pre-exegetical) biblical code of behavior. Which means they will no longer break the Sabbath by attending movies . . . That they will no longer accumulate worldly goods beyond providing for basic needs . . . the men among them will grow luxuriant beards and the women silken hair on their legs. That they will no longer engage in any sexual act other than missionary-style intercourse—and then only when procreation is the goal . . ."

—Historian Martin Duberman, as quoted by Leigh Rutledge in *Unnatural Quotations* (1988)

One response to religious anti-gay protestors at the 1993 march on Washington

disapproved (money-changers, for example), but He made no mention of homosexuals or homosexual "lifestyles."

The Federation of Parents and Friends of Lesbians and Gays (P-FLAG), a national group with a 1994 membership of thirty thousand, assembled a panel of prominent clergy and theologians to examine the Scriptures typically used against homosexuals. In the light of the cultural and chauvinistic circumstances of Bible times, the panel found no specific biblical condemnation. The group also believed that homosexuals have been the victims of a double-standard, in that most other injunctions in Leviticus are ignored today.

Recent research gives strong evidence that, in spite of rhetoric to the contrary, no one can choose their sexual orientation—homosexuality is apparently neither a choice nor the result of any num-

ber of Freudian theories, but a biologically determined phenomenon.

Homosexuals who want to settle into monogamous, committed unions are finally able to do so "in the eyes of God," through union services led by gay or gay-friendly religious authorities. While the U.S. government has yet to recognize these unions, some local governments and corporations, including AT&T, Apple Computer, Levi Strauss, and others, offer "family" benefits to same-sex families.

Many churches in traditional denominations offer outreach programs to homosexuals (often in spite of objections from some of their members). Others, including some Lutheran and Episcopal churches, have recently ordained openly gay clergy (occasionally losing members in the process). The Metropolitan Community Church, founded to provide spiritual outreach to homosexuals, has

Guilt, Crime, and Punishment

Art thou bound unto a wife? seek not to be loosed. Art thou loosed from a wife? seek not a wife.
—I Corinthians 7:27

And he arose and went: and, behold, a man of Ethiopia, an eunuch of great authority under Candace queen of the Ethiopians, who had the charge of all her treasure, and had come to Jerusalem for to worship.
—Acts 8:27

76

[T]he Bible itself . . . praises love between men (David and Jonathan), and between women (Ruth and Naomi). Genesis tells about humanity in general, but what is said there doesn't even apply to every person in the Bible. If it did, Jesus himself would have sinned by never marrying."

—Kenneth L. Cuthbertson, Ph.D.

"David and Jonathan" by Gustave Doré (1885)

"One church even said they would rather burn their church down before they sold it to us."

—Ralph Masek on the Metropolitan Community Church's difficulties in finding new facilities (1993)

over thirty thousand members; hundreds of predominantly gay churches now exist in the United States. Many Protestants and Catholics welcome gays and lesbians to their congregations, allowing them to use church rooms for meetings and discussion groups. Churches also often provide space to homosexuals of other faiths who are barred from their own churches.

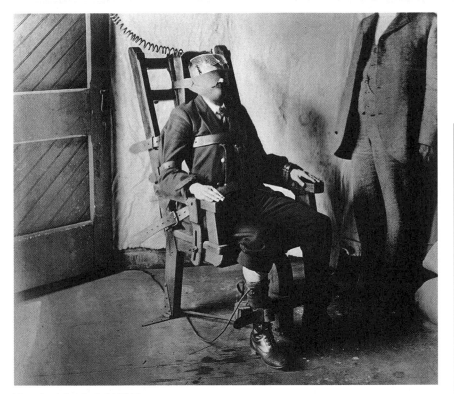

The electric chair (1908)

To Support or Oppose Capital Punishment

"An eye for an eye, a tooth for a tooth" was the brand of justice in the American Old West, just as in the Old Testament.

FRY, TED, FRY read a sign held by death penalty advocates at Ted Bundy's execution. The mother of one of Bundy's victims remarked that "he was executed on my birth-day. I guess that was my birthday present."

In the environment of the fear of crime epitomizing the late-twentieth century, capital punishment is seen both as an act of justice and as a deterrent. The public, identifying with the victim, calls for retaliation.

With the rise of Christian nations, the death penalty was typically the punishment for a variety of crimes against citizens, the

Guilt, Crime, and Punishment

SUPPORT:
Whoso sheddeth man's blood, by man shall his blood be shed: for in the image of God made he man.
—Genesis 9:6

And if any mischief follow, then thou shalt give life for life, Eye for eye, tooth for tooth, hand for hand, foot for foot, Burning for burning, wound for wound, stripe for stripe.
—Exodus 21:23–25

And if a man cause blemish in his neighbor; as he hath done, so shall it be done to him; breach for breach, eye for eye, tooth for tooth: as he hath caused a blemish in a man, so shall it be done to him again.
—Leviticus 24:19–20

For every one that curseth his father or his mother shall be surely put to death . . . And the man that committeth adultery with another man's wife, even he that committeth adultery with his neighbour's wife, the adulterer and the adulteress shall surely be put to death.
—Leviticus 20:9–10

Whosoever therefore resisteth the power, resisteth the ordinance of God: and they that resist shall receive to themselves damnation. For rulers are not a terror to good works, but to the evil. Wilt thou then not be afraid of the power? do that which is good, and thou shalt have praise of the same: For he is the minister of God to thee for good. But if thou do that which is evil, be afraid; for he beareth not the sword in vain: for he is the minister of God, a revenger to execute wrath upon him that doeth evil.

—Romans 13:2–4

Gamblers receiving their punishment. Woodcut by Albrecht Dürer (1486–1490).

state, and the church. In the early days of the church, tradition held that the means of execution fit the crime (Exodus 21:12–25). The Justinian Code (533 A.D., the first legal system established under the authority of a Christian ruler) provided that the murderer of a family member "is not put to the sword, nor to the fire, nor to any other custom-hallowed death, but is sewn in a sack with a dog, a cock, a snake, and a monkey; and, sealed in with those bestial intimates, he is thrown, as the nature of the place allows, into a nearby sea or river. In this way while he still lives he loses the use of every element; the sky is taken from him before he dies, and the earth is denied him when he is dead."

Crimes punishable by death mirrored those found in the Old Testament, with non-procreative sex or sex outside of marriage included at the top of the list.

Later, heretics and witches were burned to give them a foretaste of the flames of eternal hellfire. Those drawn and quartered were tortured before death. The body of those hanged (". . . he that is hanged is accursed of God . . ." Deuteronomy 21:23) were allowed to be left on public display—an easy way for the authorities to make a lasting point about justice ("and all Israel shall hear, and fear," Deuteronomy 13:11).

" . . . It is just possible that public sentiment is not always the expression of morality and religion."

—The Reverend W. C. de Pauley, B.D., *Punishment Human and Divine* (1925)

Technological innovations ran parallel with a gradual move to make execution more "humane" to avoid cruel and unusual punishment. The guillotine was efficient, quick, and egalitarian. Firing squads, electrocution, poisonous gas, and lethal injections demonstrate the advances of technology to hasten death.

While crucifixion, a means of capital punishment that became the symbol of a world religion, was considered a degrading form of execution, it was also considered more humane than alternatives such as impaling. Nevertheless, it offered a slow and agonizing death. Crucifixion was banned by Constantine I, the first Christian Emperor, in 337 A.D.

The martyrdom of Christians—unprotesting, unrepentant of their faith in Christ—was the ultimate proof of faith for scores of saints. In some cases, their executions were due to laws providing for capital punishment for treason or blasphemy (see the stoning of Stephen, Acts 6 and 7).

In later centuries, most notably

The Bible Tells Me So

Execution by hanging (1906)

during the Inquisition and other heresy trials, Christian authorities sought to punish individuals or groups who held blasphemous or heretical views in the eyes of the church. Unfortunates were invited to "submit for purification." Executing in the name of Christ, the church gained power, also prescribing death for crimes such as alchemy, infanticide, sexual misconduct, and sorcery. Two informants, even if unknown to the suspect, usually provided enough grounds to seize and interrogate him and initiate attempts to obtain a confession. The interrogation, which often included physical torture, was usually performed by secular authorities working on behalf of the church. If an accused heretic confessed, he may have been sentenced to minor penances such as flogging, fasts, prayers, or fines, but many cases warranted a death sentence and the confiscation of personal property. The church was not permitted to kill, however, and the accused were again turned over to secular authorities for punishment, which consisted of stretching on the rack, being burned with live coals, or, most often in cases of heresy

Guilt, Crime, and Punishment

OPPOSE:
Ye have heard that it hath been said, An eye for an eye, and a tooth for a tooth: But I say unto you, That ye resist not evil: but whosoever shall smite thee on thy right cheek, turn to him the other also. And if any man will sue thee at the law, and take away thy coat, let him have thy cloak also. And whosoever shall compel thee to go a mile, go with him twain. Give to him that asketh thee, and from him that would borrow of thee turn not thou away. Ye have heard that it hath been said, Thou shalt love thy neighbour, and hate thine enemy. But I say unto you, Love your enemies, bless them that curse you, do good to them that hate you, and pray for them which despitefully use you, and persecute you; That ye may be the children of your Father which is in heaven: for he maketh his sun to rise on the evil and on the good, and sendeth rain on the just and on the unjust. For if ye love them which love you, what reward have ye? do not even the publicans the same? And if ye salute your brethren only, what do ye more than others? do not even the publicans so? Be ye therefore perfect, even as your Father which is in heaven is perfect.
—Matthew 5:38–48

SOME OF THE OFFENSES PUNISHED BY DEATH IN THE BIBLE:

Murder
Genesis 9:6

Working on the Sabbath day
Exodus 31:15

Committing adultery (both the man and woman)
Leviticus 20:10

Men having sex with men (but not women having sex with women)
Leviticus 20:13

Children disrespecting or cursing parents
Leviticus 20:9

Children who are gluttons or drunks
Deuteronomy 21:18-23

Incest
Leviticus 20:11

Having sex with a daughter-in-law
Leviticus 20:12

Having sex with a mother-in-law
Leviticus 20:14

Men or women having sex with animals
Leviticus 20:15-16

Practicing witchcraft
Exodus 22:18; Leviticus 20:27

Coitus interruptus or masturbation
Genesis 38:7-10

OPPOSE:
And the scribes and Pharisees brought unto him a woman taken in adultery; and when they had set her in the midst, They say unto him, Master, this woman was taken in adultery, in the very act. Now Moses in the law commanded us, that such should be stoned: but what sayest thou? This they said, tempting him, that they might have to accuse him . . . So when they continued asking him, he lifted up himself, and said unto them, He that is without sin among you, let him first cast a stone at her . . . And they which heard it, being convicted by their own conscience, went out one by one, beginning at the eldest, even unto the last: and Jesus was left alone, and the woman standing in the midst.

—John 8:3–7, 9

and witchcraft, burning at the stake.

The execution of heretics evolved into the execution of witches. The practice of witchcraft in England and the New World was considered a felony rather than heresy.

In the United States, death by hanging and firing squad were the preferred methods of execution until the development of the electric chair in 1890. Nineteen twenty-four saw the first use of the gas chamber, and lethal injection gained prominence in the 1980s. Hanging is still the statutory method of capital punishment in Washington, Delaware, Montana, and New Hampshire.

Opponents of the death penalty feel that murder is murder, whether committed by an individual or by the state. The covenant with God changed from the "law" of the Old Testament to the "grace and forgiveness" of the New (Matthew 5:38–48). In 1992, when Congress ordered that a death penalty initiative be put on the bal-

The Bible Tells Me So

lot in the District of Columbia, forty-eight prominent members of the clergy opposed it.

Although studies repeatedly show no correlation between the death penalty and the murder rate, death penalty supporters simply mention Sam Berkowitz, Charles Manson, and other killers who are still alive in prison, burdening taxpayers, while the families of their victims suffer. There is little or no doubt of their guilt, and many murderers admit that, given the opportunity, they would kill again. Others have asked to be executed, defying the efforts of death penalty opponents.

Religious death penalty advocates have cited Romans 13 to show the authority of the state as "a revenger to execute wrath upon him that doeth evil." Many Christians have come to the same conclusion as Dr. William H. Baker, theologian at Moody Bible College: the death penalty is an "unpleasant necessity."

In political campaigns and in Congress, the death penalty is quickly called upon to prove that "something" can be done to deal with the crime problem, but it functions here more as a political tool than as a real threat to criminals.

In November 1993, retiring Supreme Court Justice Harry A. Blackmun stated, "I'm not sure the death penalty as administered is fairly administered . . . [there are] disturbing statistics that come in when one considers race. . . . And, of course, some people can rationalize that to their satisfaction. . . . "

The public, almost theatrical aspect of executions reflects some of the psychological dynamics of capital punishment. It was a way to set an example for the entire community, to make a point about breaking the law. But execution also satisfies a deeply rooted human need for revenge. In biblical times, members of the community often carried out the death sentence themselves by picking up a handful of rocks and stoning a criminal to death. There were no private chambers or designated executioners.

The Old Testament prescribed death for a specific list of sins; the New Testament spoke instead of spiritual suffering and abandonment, with eternal punishment in the afterlife.

In his sermons, Jesus overturned the injunctions of Exodus and Leviticus. Those who tried to trick him into heresy brought a condemned adulterous woman and essentially invited him to join them in killing her.

Jesus refused to pick up a stone.

Impaling was at one time a common means of execution. This device apparently quadrupled the executioner's efficiency.

Now the Spirit speaketh expressly, that in the latter times some shall depart from the faith, giving heed to seducing spirits, and doctrines of devils; Speaking lies in hypocrisy; having their conscience seared with a hot iron; Forbidding to marry, and commanding to abstain from meats, which God hath created to be received with thanksgiving of them which believe and know the truth. For every creature of God is good, and nothing to be refused, if it be received with thanksgiving: For it is sanctified by the word of God and prayer.

—I Timothy 4:1–5

And what agreement hath the temple of God with idols? for ye are the temple of the living God; as God hath said, I will dwell in them, and walk in them; and I will be their God, and they shall be my people.

—II Corinthians 6:16

To Mistrust and Persecute Catholics

The Bible has been used to emphasize obvious differences between Catholics and Protestants, and to prove the "alien" nature of Catholics, seen as a threat to the American way of life. Allegedly, the ultimate loyalty of all Catholics was to the pope in Rome.

Martin Luther referred to the pope as the antichrist (1 John 2:18) and to Rome (i.e., the Vatican) as Babylon. (This continues today—computer bulletin boards now carry "proof" of Catholic villainy, in the form of a file explaining how various words describing the Vatican add up to the Number of the Beast—666.)

American Protestants, accustomed to their own stark churches, spoke of what they perceive to be "idols" in Catholic churches (II Corinthians 6:16 and I John 5:21). Catholics don't eat meat on

St. Peter and St. Paul's Cathedral

Fridays and instead of preachers have priests, who aren't allowed to marry (I Timothy 4:1-5). They worship Mary and the saints, not just God or Jesus (Matthew 4:10). And

"History reveals the priest and the confessional box as enemies of virtue . . . Many parents in the past have placed their daughters in convents . . . Many a noble woman has entered the walls of Rome to escape the snares of the world, only to find that she had entered a trap to fall a victim of the seducing priest. Yet Protestant people continue to send their girls to these cesspools of iniquity."

—From *Priest and Woman: A Book for Wives, Mothers and Daughters,* compiled by Mrs. William Lloyd Clark (early 1900s)

SHALL IT COME TO THIS?

ROMISH INTOLERANCE MUST NOT TRIUMPH!

"DANGER IN THE DARK"

IS DESTINED TO BE READ BY EVERY AMERICAN.

THE AIM OF POPE PIUS IX.
"BEWARE! THERE IS DANGER IN THE DARK!"

In this illustration, Pope Pius IX destroys the constitution after having stabbed the American eagle. From an ad for *Danger in the Dark,* a "distinguished book" revealing "anti-Republican Romanism!" (1855)

Little children, keep yourselves from idols. Amen.

—I John 5:21

And call no man your father upon the earth: for one is your Father, which is in heaven.

—Matthew 23:9

For there shall arise false Christs, and false prophets, and shall shew great signs and wonders; insomuch that, if it were possible, they shall deceive the very elect.

—Matthew 24:24

Little children, it is the last time: and as ye have heard that antichrist shall come, even now are there many antichrists; whereby we know that it is the last time.

—I John 2:18

Then saith Jesus unto him, Get thee hence, Satan: for it is written, Thou shalt worship the Lord thy God, and him only shalt thou serve.

—Matthew 4:10

they always defer to their Holy Father, the pope, way over in Rome (Matthew 23:9).

For generations, questions were brought up in Sunday School and sermons. Where do you find purgatory or limbo in the Bible?

Where is there anything about a pope? Where does Jesus tell us to fast? Many of these issues were about what was *not* in the Bible. Catholics even have a different Bible (not the King James Version), were enemies of Protestant mis-

Guilt, Crime, and Punishment

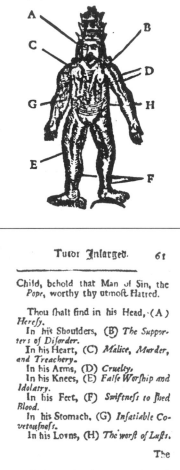

The POPE, or Man of Sin:

A
B
C
D
G
H
E
F

Tutor Inlarged.   6t

Child, behold that Man of Sin, the
Pope, worthy thy utmost Hatred.

Thou shalt find in his Head, (A)
Heresy.
In his Shoulders, (B) The Suppor-
ters of Disorder.
In his Heart, (C) Malice, Murder,
and Treachery.
In his Arms, (D) Cruelty.
In his Knees, (E) False Worship and
Idolatry.
In his Feet, (F) Swiftness to shed
Blood.
In his Stomach, (G) Insatiable Co-
vetousness.
In his Loins, (H) The worst of Lusts.

The

"The Pope, or Man of Sin" from "New
England Primer": "Child, behold that
Man of Sin, the Pope, worthy of thy
utmost Hatred. Thou shalt find in his
Head, Heresy . . . In his Heart, Malice,
Murder and Treachery . . . In his Knees,
False Worship and Idolatry. In his Feet,
Swiftness to shed Blood . . . In his
Loins, The worst of Lusts . . ."
(eighteenth century).

"There is no power but from God. The right of command, however, is not in itself linked to any one form of government. One or the other form the commonwealth may rightfully give to itself, provided such be really promotive of the common welfare . . . No reason is there why the Church should prefer one form of government to another, provided the form that is chosen be just in itself and favorable to the common good. Therefore, the rules of justice being duly observed, the people are free to adopt that form of government which befits their temper, or best accords with their traditions and customs."

—Pope Leo XIII as quoted by Most Reverend John Ireland, D.D., in a 1913 address

sionaries, and "Good Lord, do they have big families. They'll take over."

From the days of the Founding Fathers, there was concern about the loyalty of Catholics to their new country, a perceived threat of "popery" and their ultimate allegiance to a foreign potentate. They were welcomed, but not without some conditions. In 1789, George Washington formally addressed the Catholics of the United States, saying, "May the members of your society in America, animated alone by the pure spirit of Christianity, and still conducting themselves as the faithful subjects of our free government, enjoy every temporal and spiritual felicity."

In 1834, an anti-Catholic mob burned the Ursuline Convent in Charlestown, Massachusetts, in retribution for the alleged kidnapping of a young woman. A Catholic chapel in Dorchester, Massachusetts, was blown up on July 4, 1854. In the mid-1850s, Catholic churches in both Sydney and Massillon, Ohio, New York, Philadelphia, and Louisville, among other places, were mobbed, defaced, or burned, leaving many dead or injured. The violence was anti-Irish as well as anti-Catholic, incited by members of the Know-Nothing party, which fought to exclude Catholics and immigrants from public office. Originally a secret society, its members replied, "I don't know," when asked about the organization.

In 1841, the Bible was the focal point of a major political campaign. While the Protestant King James Version was read aloud in the public schools of the state of New York, as was the case in most states, Catholics sought to replace it with theirs in schools attended mostly by Catholic children. And they favored the use of public funds for Catholic schools. A Catholic ticket was formed. And defeated.

In the late nineteenth century, the American Protective Association, founded to oppose unrestricted immigration, gained momentum, providing fertile ground for more anti-Catholic rhetoric.

In the 1920s, the Ku Klux Klan added Catholics to their list of threats to white Protestant supremacy. America, they said, was Protestant from birth, the home of "Nordic" peoples. For many, being a Protestant was equated with being a true American.

In the early '50s, President Harry Truman found himself caught in the middle of the controversy over diplomatic recognition of the Vatican. One Sunday morning at the First Baptist Church in Washington, D.C., the minister angered the president by preaching against this policy. Truman walked out.

Now, as then, Baptists as a body see no justification for extending diplomatic status to the leader of one particular religious group. They had an unlikely ally in the pulpit at All Souls Church, Unitarian, of Washington, D.C. In his sermon of October 28, 1951, the Reverend A. Powell Davies preached that the fact that the Catholic leadership's ability to "reduce a Congressman to silence

is the next thing to a miracle. But the Roman clergy, less with the aid of God than of the President of the United States, have performed this quasi-miracle. It is certainly not because they have nothing to say that our Congressmen are silent. Many of them would like to say approximately what I am saying, here, this morning, but they do not dare. They are prisoners of intimidation . . . Any person in the United States government who recognizes the Vatican as a state, and the Pope as a head of state, violates the intent of the United States Constitution and betrays the principles upon which the Republic was founded."

This controversy continues today. At the UN World Conference on Population and Development in 1994, the Vatican dominated, bringing the focus of the conference to the issue of abortion.

The Catholic Church in America is currently allied on many issues with conservative Christian and fundamentalist organizations, having common objectives relating to abortion, gay rights, public funds for church-sponsored schools, and issues affecting the family.

"The United States . . . has been flooded with hordes of foreigners, many of whom are uneducated Roman Catholics, and who, from infancy, have yielded implicit obedience to the Pope . . . [the Catholic Church] has attacked our public schools . . . denounced our Bible . . . favored the union of church and state . . . thrust her hand into our treasury . . . controls our telegraphic system; she censures and subsidizes the public press; she manipulates many of our political conventions; she rules many of our large cities; . . . she has muzzled the mouths of many of our ablest statesmen, editors and ministers; she has plotted to destroy our Government; she has made her subjects swear allegiance to a foreign power . . . the claim that she has done some good does not prevent us from seeing the evils that have followed in her footsteps."

—Disciples of Christ minister John L. Brandt, concerned about a "Catholic conspiracy" (1895)

Part Five

The Way Things Ought to Be

And when thou prayest, thou shalt not be as the hypocrites are: for they love to pray standing in the synagogues and in the corners of the streets, that they may be seen of men. Verily, I say unto you, They have their reward. But thou, when thou prayest, enter into thy closet, and when thou hast shut thy door, pray to thy Father which is in secret; and thy Father which seeth in secret shall reward thee openly.

—Matthew 6:5–6

"Too Numerous to Mention." The Mormon Church dissolved its standard of polygamy, condemned as the "Mormonistic ulcer," in 1890.

> Wherefore they are no more twain, but one flesh. What therefore God hath joined together, let not man put asunder.
>
> —Matthew 19:6
>
> Wives, submit yourselves unto your own husbands, as unto the Lord. For the husband is the head of the wife, even as Christ is the head of the church: and he is the saviour of the body. Therefore as the church is subject unto Christ, so let the wives be to their own husbands in every thing. Husbands, love your wives, even as Christ also loved the church, and gave himself for it: That he might sanctify and cleanse it with the washing of water by the word.
>
> —Ephesians 5:22–26
>
> So ought men to love their wives as their own bodies. He that loveth his wife loveth himself.
>
> —Ephesians 5:28

To Define the Terms of Marriage

The Bible presents specific guidelines that have paralleled, or been the basis for, laws concerning marriage for centuries.

Among Protestants, marriage constitutes a lifelong commitment in the eyes of God. For Catholics, marriage is a sacrament: a Legal marriage consummated by sexual intercourse can be ended only when one of the partners dies. A secular legal divorce is not legitimate in the eyes of God.

In the United States, ministers, priests, and rabbis are authorized to conduct legally recognized marriage ceremonies, although a license is still required. Societal changes in recent decades have threatened the ideal marriage as biblically described. Adherents to the Scriptural definition have fought to preserve the traditional family, opposing changes that would provide legal protection and equality rights for domestic partnerships not recognized by many Christian leaders.

On this issue, the Bible is clear. Marriage should be a commitment for life between a male and a female (Mark 10:6-9). The man should be the head of the household, the woman submissive (Ephesians 5:22-26). One should marry rather than risk promiscuity

> " . . . the Lord told me it's flat none of your business . . ."
>
> —Evangelist Jimmy Swaggart to his congregation after he was embroiled in a second sex scandal involving a prostitute. This time, there were no public tears. (1991)

(I Corinthians 7:9). There is justification for shotgun weddings as well as a provision for literally paying for promiscuity (Exodus 22:16-17). In New Testament times, it was believed that, in view of the imminent return of Christ, one should remain in the same marital state—married or single—as when one came to Christianity (I Corinthians 7:20).

The rallying point for conservative Christian movements is the battle cry of "family values," which they define biblically: a family does not consist of cohabitating heterosexuals ("living in sin"), monogamous homosexual couples, or women with children who have decided, for whatever reasons, against having a husband. Marriage is a structure given by God. These Christians believe changes in secular laws giving equal rights to alternative families will constitute approval—reflecting and promoting changes in attitudes, providing the justification to ignore biblical family values.

But those targeted by the highly organized, well-financed conservative Christian movement for family values believe that they also constitute legitimate families. A popular bumper sticker reads, HATE IS NOT A FAMILY VALUE, reflecting the atmosphere of polarization, fear, and rage.

Gradually, divorce has become more accepted. A majority of Americans found it moral to elect a previously divorced man, Ronald Reagan, as president in 1980 and again in 1984.

Although the Catholic Church does not recognize secular divorce, a marriage can be dissolved by annulment, which determines that the holy union was invalid in the first place (preferably because no sexual intercourse occurred). Protestants can justify divorce when the serious sin of fornication is involved (Matthew 5:32).

In the Old Testament, a man could initiate a divorce from his wife (Deuteronomy 24:1–2), but there were no provisions for a wife to divorce her husband. In the New Testament, a woman is advised to make every effort to stand by her man, even if he is an unbeliever (I Corinthians 7:13–14): "But if the unbelieving depart, let him depart. A brother or a sister is not under bondage in such cases: but God hath called us to peace. For what knowest thou, O wife, whether thou shalt save thy husband? or how knowest thou, O man, whether thou shalt save thy wife?" (I Corinthians 7:15–16) In every other circumstance, divorce is to be avoided at all costs (I Corinthians 7:8–11).

Henry the Eighth of England proclaimed that God was displeased with his marriage because his wife bore him no male heir. The Vatican refused to declare an annulment, so he established the Church of England, breaking with Rome. A law was passed to grant his divorce.

Many feel that the acceptance of "casual" divorce mocks the institution of marriage and contributes to the current "crisis" in family values. It damages families, particularly children. And from a biblical perspective, it constitutes adultery (Matthew 19:9, Mark 10:12), a crime specifically forbidden (Exo-

The first self-described "born again" president, Jimmy Carter admitted in a 1976 *Playboy* interview to having "looked on a lot of women with lust. I've committed adultery in my heart many times." For his honesty about an absolutely innocuous transgression by today's standards, he was often severely ridiculed.

But from the beginning of the creation God made them male and female. For this cause shall a man leave his father and mother, and cleave to his wife; And they twain shall be one flesh: so then they are no more twain, but one flesh. What therefore God hath joined together, let not man put asunder.
—Mark 10:6–9

I say therefore to the unmarried and widows, It is good for them if they abide even as I. But if they cannot contain, let them marry: for it is better to marry than to burn. And unto the married I command, yet not I, but the Lord, Let not the wife depart from her husband: But and if she depart, let her remain unmarried, or be reconciled to her husband: and let not the husband put away his wife.
—I Corinthians 7:8–11

And the woman which hath an husband that believeth not, and if he be pleased to dwell with her, let her not leave him. For the unbelieving husband is sanctified by the wife, and the unbelieving wife is sanctified by the husband: else were your children unclean; but now are they holy.
—I Corinthians 7:13–14

"It's in the Bible."

—Polygamist Elwood Gallimore, Martinsville, Virginia, during his trial for polygamy in 1993. He expected a returning Jesus to show up in court and defend him (the Second Coming was due two months after his court date was set).

Let every man abide in the same calling wherein he was called.
—I Corinthians 7:20

But I say unto you, That whosoever shall put away his wife, saving for the cause of fornication, causeth her to commit adultery: and whosoever shall marry her that is divorced committeth adultery.
—Matthew 5:32

Thou shalt not commit adultery.
—Exodus 20:14

dus 20:14) and punishable by death for both participants (Leviticus 20:10). With relaxed divorce laws, one can legally have many wives or husbands—just not at the same time. To many, this can be viewed as the legal sanction of sequential polygamy.

Polygamy, generally used in reference to a man who has two or more wives simultaneously, has been a distinguishing component of many biblically based Christian groups. (Today, most of these are defined as cults.) Some have even rationalized multiple sex partners, often including minors, for their leaders. In a few cases polygamy is the only legally objectionable practice advocated by an otherwise "acceptable" fundamentalist religious group. In such cases, the Old Testament is called into play as justification for what is defined as a "religious practice" among consenting adults.

God did provide specific instructions for taking a second wife as the spoils of war (Deuteronomy 21: 11–14). David had two wives (I Samuel 27:3), but he's not a good

role model, having committed adultery with the wife of Uriah (II Samuel 11). God was not particularly pleased with King Solomon's obsession with "many strange women" and the fact that he had "seven hundred wives, princesses,

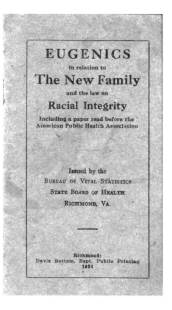

Cover of booklet intended for public health workers in Virginia, including details on the new law on miscegenation. Published by the Bureau of Vital Statistics, State Board of Health, Richmond, Virginia, 1924.

WHAT MISCEGENATION IS!

—AND—

W H A T   W E   A R E   T O   E X P E C T

Now that Mr. Lincoln is Re-elected.

The threat of miscegenation used as a political tool. Title page of a book by L. Seaman, LL.D. (1864)

and three hundred concubines" (I Kings 11:1–3).

During the nineteenth century in America, members of the Church of Jesus Christ of Latter-Day Saints practiced polygamy. In 1890, their leader, Wilford Woodruff, abolished the practice. Polygamy was also found in small Christian utopian communities.

Miscegenation, or mixed-race marriage, is usually defined as marriage between whites and non-whites, particularly blacks. At one time, laws against miscegenation were enforced in as many as thirty states. An 1883 Supreme Court decision determined that since both black and white partners were prosecuted in an equal manner, the law did not discriminate.

In 1959, Judge Leon Bazile of Caroline County, Virginia, ruling in the case of the marriage of construction worker Richard Loving (white) and Mildred Jeter Loving (of black and Native American heritage) stated that "Almighty God created the races white, black, yellow, Malay and red, and he placed them on separate continents. The fact that he separated the races shows that he did not intend for the races to mix."

Perhaps he based his argument on the story of the Tower of Babel, in which God scattered the frustrated architects "abroad from thence upon the face of all the earth . . ." (Genesis 11:8), coupled with his interpretation of the curse Moses put upon the descendants of Ham. The division of races that he cited had at one time been acceptable scientific fact, and was specifically mentioned in the 1924 law he was enforcing. Judge Bazile certainly didn't remember the sad fate of Miriam, punished with leprosy after she "spake against Moses because of the Ethiopian woman whom he had married" (Numbers 12:1).

In June 1967, the case of *Loving* v. *The State of Virginia* was heard by the Supreme Court. All nine justices reached the decision that such laws are unconstitutional—a clear-cut decision on racial equality.

"And the spirit of jealousy come upon him, and he be jealous of his wife, and she be defiled; or if the spirit of jealousy come upon him, and he be jealous of his wife, and she be not defiled [The husband takes his wife to a priest, who makes her drink a potion that includes dust from the temple floor.] Then the priest shall charge the woman with an oath of cursing . . . [and say] And this water that causeth the curse shall go into thy bowels, to make thy belly to swell, and thy thigh to rot . . . Then shall the man be guiltless from iniquity, and this woman shall bear her iniquity."— Numbers 5:14–31

—A rarely cited passage of Scripture that some authors on the subject of spouse abuse have suggested is a biblical justification for the harsh treatment of women by their husbands

Drink no longer water, but use a little wine for thy stomach's sake and thine often infirmities.

—I Timothy 5:23

The Son of man came eating and drinking, and they say, Behold a man gluttonous, and a winebibber, a friend of publicans and sinners. But wisdom is justified of her children.

—Matthew 11:19

Belshazzar the king made a great feast to a thousand of his lords, and drank wine before the thousand . . . Then they brought the golden vessels that were taken out of the temple of the house of God which was at Jerusalem; and the king, and his princes, his wives, and his concubines, drank in them. They drank wine, and praised the gods of gold, and of silver, of brass, of iron, of wood, and of stone.

—Daniel 5:1, 3–4

" . . . we believe it to be our duty to support for office such candidates as are in favor of temperance reform . . ."

—A resolution of the Baptist Mississippi Convention (1884)

To Control the Consumption of Alcohol

In the late 1800s, the Women's Christian Temperance Union formed the Anti-Saloon League of America to fight the loose morals and godlessness of the nation through a national campaign to outlaw drinking. By January 1920, the 18th Amendment to the Constitution had gone into effect, prohibiting the manufacture, sale, and transportation of alcoholic beverages.

Prohibition found both support and opposition. And each point of view was validated by the same Bible.

The debate over Prohibition was not simply between "drys" and "wets." It pitted rural against urban, American-born Protestant against immigrant Roman Catholic, fundamentalist against intellectual.

At its peak, sixty thousand churches were affiliated with the League, whose first lobbyist in Washington bragged that "The graves of many state legislators and members of Congress can be seen along our line of march, and there are other graves waiting."

Women in the temperance movement appeared in saloons, staging prayer meetings and sing-

"Woman is ordained to lead the vanguard of this great movement."— Frances E. Willard, founder of the Women's Christian Temperance Union (1874). The movement gained greater strength when the cause became one of social justice, focusing on the drunken father and the tragedies of spouse abuse, child abuse, and poverty. With Bibles in the hands of its proponents, the movement became known as The Woman's Holy War.

ins, with music such as "The Moderate Drinker" ("Moderate drinker! O beware, Satan spreads a dreadful net . . ."), "Oh Water for Me," and "Ode to Rum" ("Pocket emptier, Sabbath breaker, Conscience stifler, Guilt's recourse"). "Mother of the Crusade," Mrs. E. F. Thompson, believed ". . . the truth in [temperance hymns] touches the heart of the hearer unawares, when he is not on the defensive against the gospel."

Left: Women temperance protesters depicted as "Jewels Among Swine" in an engraving by Thomas Nast for *Harper's Weekly* (1874)

93

The women recounted many stories of the conversions of saloon-keepers, distillers, and customers.

Chicago White Stockings baseball-player-turned-Presbyterian-minister Billy Sunday championed the cause of Prohibition, traveling the country to promote water as a replacement for alcohol. Buttermilk was also recommended.

The Baptist, Methodist, Presbyterian, and Congregational churches were the main forces

Wine is a mocker, strong drink is raging: and whosoever is deceived thereby is not wise.
—Proverbs 20:1

It is not for kings, O Lemuel, it is not for kings to drink wine; nor for princes strong drink: Lest they drink, and forget the law, and pervert the judgment of any of the afflicted.
—Proverbs 31:4–5

But they also have erred through wine, and through strong drink are out of the way; the priest and the prophet have erred through strong drink, they are swallowed up of wine . . . they err in vision, they stumble in judgment.
—Isaiah 28:7

And also that every man should eat and drink, and enjoy the good of all his labour, it is the gift of God.
—Ecclesiastes 3:13

Who hath woe? who hath sorrow? who hath contentions? who hath babbling? who hath wounds without cause? who hath redness of eyes? They that tarry long at the wine; they that go to seek mixed wine. Look not thou upon the wine when it is red, when it giveth his colour in the cup, when it moveth itself aright. At the last it biteth like a serpent, and stingeth like an adder.

—Proverbs 23:29–32

And in this mountain shall the Lord of hosts make unto all people a feast of fat things, a feast of wines on the lees, of fat things full of marrow, of wines on the lees well refined.

—Isaiah 25:6

"The truth is that the alcoholic evil . . . will perish forever, execrated by man and consumed in the fiercest flames of God's wrath."

—Senator Henry William Blair of New Hampshire (1887)

The Reverend Billy Sunday (1915)

behind Prohibition, with some help from the smaller Disciples of Christ, Christian Science, and Mormon groups. The Anti-Saloon League had only token support from Episcopals and Lutherans, Jews and Catholics, prompting New Hampshire senator and temperance leader Henry William Blair to warn of the "foreign element," which brings with it "un-American prejudices and customs . . ." The First World War gave a boost to the "unpatriotic" argument against drinking, because so many German-born Americans were in the alcoholic beverage business.

The Bible contains many references to wine—a source of sorrow and drunkenness as well as joy and communion. From pulpits and pamphlets, the drys used Bible stories of the escapades of Noah, Belshazzar, and the Prodigal Son to illustrate the dangers of drinking.

The wets opened their Bibles to find the great miracle of the wedding of Cana (was Jesus a bootlegger?) and the Lord's Supper, and remembered that Jesus himself

"The ballot-box is the place to do the work. Whiskey or no whiskey is the great question before us in these United States . . . But how far should the churches go in this struggle? . . . if the power held by our churches is not used for God . . . we shall be false to the high trust that the Redeemer of the world has committed to our charge."

—Sermon of H. M. Wharton, quoted by H. M. Wharton, *Gospel Talks* (1888)

Left: Seventeenth-century engraving of the biblical wedding at Cana

was accused of being a drunkard by those who attacked his ministry toward outcasts (Matthew 11:19).

The 1920s saw widespread avoidance of the new temperance laws by otherwise law-abiding people, many having ethnic or cultural traditions involving alcohol. Nightclubs and saloons were replaced by the speakeasy. The lack of legally available alcoholic beverages also promoted the rise of organized criminal groups and gang warfare involving black-market manufacture and distribution.

Government-appointed "revenuers" routinely destroyed illegal alcohol caches. Here, over seven hundred cases of beer were destroyed. Philadelphia, 1923.

The Way Things Ought to Be

The Great Depression found fanatical wets blaming Prohibition for the country's problems: millions out of work in brewing and distilling; agricultural losses due to a decreased demand for fermentable grains and fruit; costs of new criminal activities and increased law enforcement; and the loss of federal revenue through taxes on alcoholic beverages.

Patriotism—and jobs for Americans in the face of the Depression—was part of the justification for passing the 21st Amendment, repealing Prohibition, in 1933.

Most who study this period conclude that the drys were unwilling to examine the difference between wine and hard liquor, between drinking and drunkenness, or to distinguish this issue from their growing xenophobia, preferring instead to promote abstinence alone in a prime example of "single issue" politics.

When the ruler of the feast had tasted the water that was made wine, and knew not whence it was: (but the servants which drew the water knew;) the governor of the feast called the bridegroom, And saith unto him, Every man at the beginning doth set forth good wine; and when men have well drunk, then that which is worse; but thou has kept the good wine until now. This beginning of miracles did Jesus in Cana of Galilee, and manifested forth his glory; and his disciples believed on him.
—John 2:9–11

And as they were eating, Jesus took bread, and blessed it, and brake it, and gave it to the disciples, and said, Take, eat; this is my body. And he took the cup, and gave thanks, and gave it to them, saying, Drink ye all of it; For this is my blood of the new testament, which is shed for many for the remission of sins. But I say unto you, I will not drink henceforth of this fruit of the vine, until that day when I drink it new with you in my Father's kingdom.
—Matthew 26:26–29

And he said unto them, When ye pray, say, Our Father which art in heaven, Hallowed be thy name. Thy kingdom come. Thy will be done, as in heaven, so in earth. Give us day by day our daily bread. And forgive us our sins; for we also forgive every one that is indebted to us. And lead us not into temptation; but deliver us from evil.

—Luke 11:2–4

After this manner therefore pray ye: Our Father which art in heaven, Hallowed be thy name. Thy kingdom come. Thy will be done in earth, as it is in heaven. Give us this day our daily bread. And forgive us our debts, as we forgive our debtors. And lead us not into temptation, but deliver us from evil: For thine is the kingdom, and the power, and the glory, for ever. Amen.

—Matthew 6:9–13

Even so faith, if it hath not works, is dead, being alone.

—James 2:17

For as the body without the spirit is dead, so faith without works is dead also.

—James 2:26

As Part of a Program of Recovery from Addiction

A strong spiritual awakening was instrumental in the recovery of "Bill W.," who also discovered that helping others to recover was a key to his own sobriety. His chance meeting with "Dr. Bob" in Akron, Ohio, who had recently become acquainted with the Oxford Group, began a movement that, as of 1994, numbers over 89,000 groups, with AA activity in 141 countries.

The Oxford Group was a nondenominational spiritual movement that sought to regain the first-century power of Christianity in the twentieth century, by "making a surrender to God through rigorous self-examination, confessing their character defects to another human being, making restitution for harm done to others, and giving without thought of reward." All guidance came from God, with a heavy reliance on the Scriptures. Founded by F. N. D. Buchman, the group also came to be known as Moral Rearmament.

Dr. Bob Smith, an alcoholic, met with the Akron, Ohio, Oxford Group in 1933. Dr. Bob, and fellow sober alcoholic Bill Wilson, borrowed principles of the Oxford Group to create a program to help other alcoholics remain sober. The new group used continuous contact and interaction with fellow

> "God, grant me the Serenity to accept the things I cannot change, Courage to change the things I can, and Wisdom to know the difference."
>
> —The Serenity Prayer (Anonymous), often a part of recovery programs

alcoholics to achieve a goal of focusing the alcoholic's energy toward helping another maintain sobriety.

Early members of this fellowship found recovery guidelines similar to their own reflected in the biblical Epistle of James: humility and taking recovery "one day at a time" (James 4:14–15); the importance of prayer and "confession" (compare to "qualifying" and "sharing" in AA) (James 5:16); and service to others (James 2:17, 2:26).

Alcoholics Anonymous was the first of many recovery programs based on the Twelve Steps. These programs are used to end or manage addictions and obsessions relating to alcohol, drugs, sex, food, and smoking. The original group spawned other groups that aid recovery for those affected by alcoholic family members or spouses.

Alcoholics Anonymous has found support from both the medical and the religious communities, in spite of the fact that the group is not specifically Bible- or Christ-centered. Members are asked to focus on a Higher Power, to whom they relinquish themselves. The term Higher Power may also have derived from the work of psychologist William James, who lectured that "the presence of a higher and friendly Power seems to be the fundamental feature in the spiritual life" (1902).

Few can argue that most drunks don't respond to being preached at. But many have found their way back to the religion of their childhoods, often after being disenchanted with, threatened by, or overdosed on an established religion. For many, the meetings become the center of their spiritual lives—the only place they have ever found offering unconditional, nonjudgmental acceptance.

Twelve Step groups strongly encourage participation in church and religion.

Prophetically, the founders of AA imagined a worldwide interest in the program, which now also includes Muslims, those practicing Eastern religions, agnostics, and atheists.

In an individual program of recovery, some may develop a relationship with their Higher Power involving prayer for specific outcomes or material objects, but this is not at the basis of the program.

Blessed are the poor in spirit: for theirs is the kingdom of heaven. Blessed are they that mourn: for they shall be comforted. Blessed are the meek: for they shall inherit the earth. Blessed are they which do hunger and thirst after righteousness: for they shall be filled. Blessed are the merciful: for they shall obtain mercy. Blessed are the pure in heart: for they shall see God. Blessed are the peacemakers: for they shall be called the children of God. Blessed are they which are persecuted for righteousness' sake: for theirs is the kingdom of heaven. Blessed are ye, when men shall revile you, and persecute you, and shall say all manner of evil against you falsely, for my sake. Rejoice, and be exceeding glad: for great is your reward in heaven: for so persecuted they the prophets which were before you.

—Matthew 5:3–12

Let every soul be subject unto the higher powers. For there is no power but of God: the powers that be are ordained of God.

—Romans 13:1

The Way Things Ought to Be

Whereas ye know not what shall be on the morrow. For what is your life? It is even a vapour, that appeareth for a little time, and then vanisheth away. For that ye ought to say, If the Lord will, we shall live, and do this, or that.

—James 4:14–15

Confess your faults one to another, and pray one for another, that ye may be healed. The effectual fervent prayer of a righteous man availeth much.

—James 5:16

NIGHT. **MORNING.**

In this nineteenth-century caricature, a drinker is beset by devils to create the punitive hangover.

"In medical language, I consider drunkenness, strictly speaking, to be a disease, produced by a remote cause, and giving birth to actions and movements in the living body that disorder the functions of health."

—Edinburgh physician Thomas Trotter, 1804. The comment upset the church, as it (and most doctors) viewed "inebrity" as a sin, and considered most alcoholics incurables of the lower classes.

The Serenity Prayer concerns turning over control, not taking it. The recovering person admits powerlessness, and finds unconditional love and acceptance coming from the Higher Power of his or her understanding.

Serenity was defined as "true, interior soul-peace" in Emmet Fox's *The Sermon on the Mount: The Key to Success in Life* (1930s), in which Fox interpreted the Beatitudes of Matthew 5 and The Lord's Prayer. Bill W. became aware of the Serenity Prayer when he read it in an obituary column. The final version used in AA is the opening of the 1934 Serenity Prayer by American theologian Reinhold Niebuhr, but Twelve Step programs frequently refer to the author as "anonymous."

Many Alcoholics Anonymous meetings throughout the United States utilize both the Serenity Prayer and The Lord's Prayer.

Biblically based Twelve Step programs have now been introduced specifically to help Christians.

"Now will you be good?" 1908 cartoon, New York *Herald*.

And he said unto them, This is that which the Lord hath said, To morrow is the rest of the holy sabbath unto the Lord: bake that which ye will bake to day, and seethe that ye will seethe; and that which remaineth over lay up for you to be kept until the morning.

—Exodus 16:23

Remember the sabbath day, to keep it holy. Six days shalt thou labour, and do all thy work: But the seventh day is the sabbath of the Lord thy God: in it thou shalt not do any work, thou, nor thy son, nor thy daughter, thy manservant, nor thy maidservant, nor thy cattle, nor thy stranger that is within thy gates.

—Exodus 20:8–10

To Forbid Work and Commerce on Sundays

As Christianity evolved, Sunday became the Sabbath—the Lord's day, the day Christ rose from the dead, and the day when Christians "broke bread" (Acts 20:7) and collected for the poor (I Corinthians 16:2).

The Christian Sabbath eventually came to resemble the Jewish model, with injunctions against work and commerce (the word *sabbath* comes from the Hebrew word *shabbath,* which literally means "rest"). The church, monarchs, and legislative bodies enacted laws to limit the activities of the general population on Sundays. And as breaking the laws was deemed punishable by death in the Old Testament, there were severe repercussions for violators even in the New World. Whippings or time in the stocks were prescribed pun-

"Whether a man will play golf on Sunday is a question between himself and God; he must determine whether it be a sin or not; once the State legislates against Sunday golf, the game becomes a criminal offence when indulged in on Sunday. This step the State will take only when it considers the action in question to be subversive of its good."

—The Reverend W. C. de Pauley, Society for Promoting Christian Knowledge (1925)

100

"Jesus came to send a sword in the earth as well as peace; draw your sword and strike; strike the Sunday theatre, strike the Sunday newspaper, strike the beer-garden and bar-room, strike until the last foe shall fall and die, strike for God, for religion, for happiness and heaven, and your posterity, and the nations of the earth will rise up and bless you, and the Lord, the righteous Judge, will say "WELL DONE."

—Sermon of H. M. Wharton (c 1880s), from *Gospel Talks* (1886)

Six days may work be done; but in the seventh is the sabbath of rest, holy to the Lord: whosoever doeth any work in the sabbath day, he shall surely be put to death.
—Exodus 31:15

And if the people of the land bring ware or any victuals on the sabbath day to sell, that we would not buy it of them on the sabbath, or on the holy day: and that we would leave the seventh year, and the exaction of every debt.

—Nehemiah 10:31

"Jesus and His Disciples in the Cornfield," a nineteenth-century engraving by Gustave Doré. "The sabbath was made for man, and not man for the sabbath" (Mark 2:27).

ishments. Fines were imposed by Colonial magistrates for carrying guns or working on Sundays. Casually driving a wagon could result in an indictment. Repeat violators could face execution.

The concerns of commerce and conscience collided repeatedly over what is known in the United States as "blue laws" (the term sup-

posedly coming from the blue paper on which the code of laws of Puritan New Haven were first printed). Since the seventeenth century, laws mandating a "Puritan Sabbath" have caused divisions between the faithful and unfaithful as well as within the ranks of the most devout. After all, Jesus himself made exceptions to Sabbath law (Matthew 12:1–3).

In America, blue laws were enacted on both state and local levels, some with exceptions reflecting local traditions—you could buy food, but you couldn't buy soap; you couldn't buy clothes, but you could buy a horse—raising such questions as What constitutes an emergency purchase? Who should be allowed to work?

A Supreme Court decision (*McGowan* v. *Maryland*) in 1961 accepted the religious origins of

"If a person, on a Sabbath Day, be found laboring at any trade . . . except in household or other work of necessity or charity, he shall be fined not less than $5 for each offense."

—Law in Wheeling, West Virginia (1890s)

> "We see this desecration of the Sabbath increasing every year, giving up a little here and giving up a little there. A few years ago in Chicago we did not have a theater open on the Sabbath, but now every theater is open. Every Sunday night those theaters are crowded. I want to say to the working men, if you give up the Sabbath, you give up the best friend you've got, and it will not be long before these capitalists will take your Sabbath and make you work seven days in the week, and you will not earn a dollar more than you do now in six days."
>
> —Reverend Dwight Lyman Moody, from a sermon titled "Tekel" (1890)

> At that time Jesus went on the sabbath day through the corn; and his disciples were an hungred, and began to pluck the ears of corn, and to eat. But when the Pharisees saw it, they said unto him, Behold, thy disciples do that which is not lawful to do upon the sabbath day. But he said unto them, Have ye not read what David did, when he was an hungred, and they that were with him.
>
> —Matthew 12:1–3

> And he said unto them, The sabbath was made for man, and not man for the sabbath: Therefore the Son of man is Lord also of the sabbath.
>
> —Mark 2:27–28

blue laws, but agreed that the state could set aside a "day of rest."

Blue laws may inhibit some activities, but they do not infringe on an individual's right to practice religion. Special restrictions, such as those dealing with alcohol, are now merely coincidental with religious tradition and usually left up to local governments to enforce. Their original religious intent discarded, blue laws have gradually disintegrated with changes in public attitude and an inability, or lack of interest, to enforce them.

In the 1920s, Canadian Methodist Charles H. Huestis wrote that Sunday was "a day for the home." The Sabbath, he said, was a time to spend time in the presence of the Lord and of one's family, particularly the children; it was the day to break the routine, to become refreshed and reinvigorated in mind, body, and spirit.

And today, in most cities, a reflective morning in church can be followed by an invigorating afternoon spent mowing the lawn or wandering through the mall.

"It being one chief project of the old deluder, Satan, to keep men from the knowledge of the Scriptures, . . . It is therefore ordered, that every township in this jurisdiction . . . appoint one within their town to teach all such children as shall resort to him to write and read . . ."

—Massachusetts School Law of 1647. The first system of public education in the American Colonies was established to assure that children would grow up being able to read the Bible for themselves.

To Justify or Oppose Prayer in Public Schools

The first American school system, begun in Massachusetts, 1647, was established to ensure that children would grow up with the ability to read the Bible for themselves.

American schools typically included class prayer, the reading of Bible verses, or the recitation of The Lord's Prayer as part of everyday activities until 1962. Then, concerns over separation of church and state caused the Supreme Court to rule school prayer unconstitutional, a violation of the First Amendment "establishment of religion" clause. Ever since, conservative Americans have fought for its return.

Former mathematics instructor and founder of the fundamentalist group Citizens for Excellence in Education, Robert L. Simonds sought to "win souls for Jesus Christ" in the classroom. *The Wall Street Journal* reported that "He began each lesson by projecting Scripture onto the classroom wall. When a Jewish student or Hare Krishna follower objected, he would beckon them into his office, tell them never to interrupt him again and read them more scripture." Simonds stated that he was "a member of Presi-

Title page of the *New England Primer*, eighteenth century.

dent Ronald Reagan's Task Force to Implement the National Commission on Excellence in Education Report: 'A Nation At Risk.' "

Senator Sam Ervin, former President Ronald Reagan, and others suggested a constitutional amendment to permit voluntary prayer in public schools. A number of states enacted pro-school-prayer laws, which the Supreme Court routinely overturned.

In 1984, the "equal access" law went into effect, allowing high school students to hold religious meetings on school grounds before or after school hours. Several states have introduced policies calling for a "moment of silence" at the start of the school day, raising concerns that the policies are a first step toward a return to compulsory prayer and the integration of religion and government.

In 1992, the Fifth U.S. Circuit Court of Appeals in Houston, Texas, ruled to allow student-led prayers that were "nonproselytizing and nonsectarian" to be read at graduations (*Jones* v. *Clearcreek Independent School District*). The Supreme Court did not comment on the decision and let it stand.

In 1994, following the logic of the Texas ruling, Dr. Bishop Knox, principal of Wingfield High School, Jackson, Mississippi, polled the student body, finding overwhelming support for student-led Christian school prayer. After allowing students to read a twenty-one-word prayer mentioning God, but not Jesus, over the school's public-address system, he was suspended for insubordination. Knox became a local hero and the national symbol of the cause; two months later,

the Mississippi House approved a bill permitting "non-sectarian, non-proselytizing, student-initiated" school prayers, subsequently overturned by the courts. There is no reason to doubt that the battle will continue into the next century.

Those opposed to school prayer feel that it's not the responsibility of the public schools to teach religious practices, and that students of minority religions would become a "captive audience." They would be made to feel uncomfortable,

OPPOSE:
And when thou prayest, thou shalt not be as the hypocrites are: for they love to pray standing in the synagogues and in the corners of the streets, that they may be seen of men. Verily I say unto you, They have their reward. But thou, when thou prayest, enter into thy closet, and when thou has shut thy door, pray to thy Father which is in secret; and thy Father which seeth in secret shall reward thee openly. But when ye pray, use not vain repetitions, as the heathen do: for they think that they shall be heard for their much speaking. Be not ye therefore like unto them: for your Father knoweth what things ye have need of, before ye ask him.
—Matthew 6:5–8

Be not rash with thy mouth, and let not thine heart be hasty to utter any thing before God: for God is in heaven, and thou upon earth: therefore let thy words be few.
—Ecclesiastes 5:2

"Congress shall make no law respecting an establishment of religion, or prohibiting the free exercise thereof; or abridging the freedom of speech, or of the press; or the right of the people peaceably to assemble, and to petition the government for a redress of grievances."

—The Bill of Rights (First Amendment to the Constitution), 1791. Prayer in public schools is indicative of the ongoing conflict in First Amendment issues—accommodating religion, which would violate the establishment of religion clause, and treating religion in an exclusionary way, which would violate the free exercise clause.

The public-school question: "What sectarian appropriation of the school fund is doing . . . And what it may lead to." Note the transition from a "Catholic" school to the next logical step of a school filled with "idols," which the American children are made to worship. (*Harper's Weekly*, 1873)

exposed to and influenced by views their parents may find objectionable to their own religions. They could become outcasts. And opponents also refer to many instances in our history of the use of religion to point out differences between fellow citizens, and the resulting bigotry, divisiveness, and violence.

Studies repeatedly show that a large portion of the population prays. Most school systems work consciously to avoid offending even one student with a different religious background. Yet non-praying or non-Christian students have in some cases been asked to stand outside the classroom while the rest of the class prayed together.

The challenge comes in avoiding an appearance of placing one religion above others. One solution would be to provide equal

time to all. However, among Christians, both Catholic and Protestant, views range from those of the biblical literalists to the moderates and liberals, with radically different creeds and doctrines stated or implied. Add to the mix Jews, Muslims, Native Americans, Buddhists, and variations within each faith, and you could have a recipe for chaos, leaving no time for education.

There can be no perfect ge-

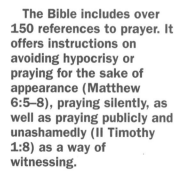

The Bible includes over 150 references to prayer. It offers instructions on avoiding hypocrisy or praying for the sake of appearance (Matthew 6:5–8), praying silently, as well as praying publicly and unashamedly (II Timothy 1:8) as a way of witnessing.

"Nothing in this constitution prohibits the free and voluntary expression of religious faith, or religious instruction and association, within the public institutions, or public schools, of the United States."

—Frequent Presidential candidate Pat Buchanan on his vision of a revised constitution (1988)

Issues of religion in schools and "family values" are hardly new. (KKK sheet music cover, 1920s)

"We were here first. You don't take our shared common values and say they are biased and bigoted . . . we are the keepers of what is right and what is wrong."

—Reverend Lou Sheldon, Traditional Values Coalition (1993)

neric prayer. And if there were, a Christian fundamentalist is unlikely to tolerate that prayer led by a Muslim fundamentalist, each believing the other already damned to eternal hellfire. The idea of collective meditation might please only the Buddhists.

A moment of silence among children is practically unheard of, and could be a mockery of the concept of prayer.

Pro-prayer adherents often see non-Christians who have worked to remove school prayer as a minority intent on removing religion from public life entirely. Many believe that the expulsion of

school prayer has contributed greatly to the increase in violence, sex, and drug use among young people by removing the guiding force that prayer can provide. Some opponents agree, but feel that freedom of religion must also provide their children freedom *from* the religions of others; that the role of religious education should be carried out at home and at church, not in public schools.

Thousands of Christian parents now opt for home schooling in order to shelter their children from negative outside influences and to assure them an entirely Christian environment.

It is repeatedly noted that students can still pray in school. They can say grace over lunch. Make the sign of the Cross before a free throw on the basketball court. Undoubtedly, many thousands of prayers are said daily before pop tests.

"[The Constitution] does not require children to leave their religion at the schoolhouse door . . . When the First Amendment is invoked as an obstacle to private expression of religion it is being misused . . . Religion has a proper place in private and a proper place in public because the public square belongs to all Americans."

—President Bill Clinton (1995)

"I hope I live to see the day when, as in the early days of our country, we won't have any public schools. The churches will have taken them over again and Christians will be running them. What a happy day that will be!"

—Jerry Falwell (1979)

Part Six

Science, Medicine, and the World

And ye shall know the truth, and the truth shall make you free.

—John 8:32

108

To Oppose or Embrace Medical Science

Scriptures have played an important role in helping man to deal with landmark events in life, including birth, serious illness, and death. But with so many previously unimaginable medical advances, the question is often raised: how and when does medical science interfere with God's intent?

On February 1, 1866, following a fall on the ice, a gravely injured Massachusetts woman requested her Bible, read the story of Jesus healing the palsied man (Matthew 9), and was immediately healed. The woman, Mary Baker Eddy, went on to found a society that eventually became known as Christian Science.

Christian Scientists use two primary written sources, the most important of which is the King James Version of the Bible. The second is Mary Baker Eddy's *Science and Health with Key to the Scriptures,* which helps Christian Scientists focus on healing and spiritual growth through prayer and an understanding of the Scriptures. For them, this is the truth that "shall make you free."

Christian Scientists typically prefer to use the power of prayer and a Christian Science practi-

Jesus healing the blind man on the Sabbath (John 9)

tioner to heal the sick (see James 5:13–15). But laws have changed, setting up some Christian Science parents for a charge of child neglect. Christian Scientists argue that they do provide treatment for medical problems—just not conventional ones, such as those prescribed by doctors.

In the case of the *Commonwealth* v. *Twitchell,* a Christian Scientist couple in Massachusetts was convicted of involuntary manslaughter in the death of their child, a charge that was subsequently overturned by the state Supreme Court. In 1993, a Minneapolis jury ordered a $5.2 million damage award against the Christian Science Church in the case of the death of an eleven-year-

Therefore Sarah laughed within herself, saying, After I am waxed old shall I have pleasure, my lord being old also? And the Lord said unto Abraham, Wherefore did Sarah laugh, saying, Shall I of a surety bear a child, which am old? Is any thing too hard for the Lord? At the time appointed I will return unto thee, according to the time of life, and Sarah shall have a son.
—Genesis 18:12–14

old. In 1994, the Centers for Disease Control reported a rate of measles infection more than four times higher than the same period in the previous year. Nearly half the afflicted were Christian Scientists.

Christian Scientists argue that secular laws infringe upon their First Amendment right to practice religion, as well as parental rights regarding their children's welfare.

Jehovah's Witnesses are reluctant to accept transfusions of blood or human blood products, based on their reading of Scripture (for example, see Leviticus 3:17 and 19:26, and Acts 15:29). They will, however, accept their own blood when stored in anticipation of a surgical procedure.

Life-saving transfusions of blood from one human to another (or, for that matter, tissue or organ transplants from other humans or animals) could hardly be conceived of in first-century Palestine, yet the Bible is nevertheless used by Jehovah's Witnesses to provide guidance in such cases. Modern medical advances pose many great questions yet to be definitively answered by the Scriptures.

In the Old Testament, childlessness was seen as a punishment. Today, the help a childless couple gets from medical science to conceive and bear a child is, to them, a miracle. Women can provide surrogate wombs, and a grandmother can carry and give birth to her own grandchild. And women over the age of sixty can, through scientific advancement, have a child—making them modern-day Sarahs (Genesis 18:12–14). European governments have moved to regulate these procedures.

On the other extreme of life is death. Should doctors use extraordinary means to prolong life, regardless of the quality that particular life will have, or should the family or patient herself have the

An engraving memorializing priests who died tending and ministering to plague victims in Italy

Is any among you afflicted? let him pray. Is any merry? let him sing psalms. Is any sick among you? let him call for the elders of the church; and let them pray over him, anointing him with oil in the name of the Lord: And the prayer of faith shall save the sick, and the Lord shall raise him up; and if he have committed sins, they shall be forgiven him.
—James 5:13–15

That ye abstain from meats offered to idols, and from blood, and from things strangled, and from fornication: from which if ye keep yourselves, ye shall do well. Fare ye well.
—Acts 15:29

And the Lord visited Sarah as he had said, and the Lord did unto Sarah as he had spoken. For Sarah conceived, and bare Abraham a son in his old age, at the set time of which God had spoken to him. And Abraham called the name of his son that was born unto him, whom Sarah bare to him, Isaac.
—Genesis 21:1–3

110

And he said unto them, Ye will surely say unto me this proverb, Physician, heal thyself: whatsoever we have heard done in Capernaum, do also here in thy country.
—Luke 4:23

Ye shall not eat any thing with the blood: neither shall ye use enchantment, nor observe times.
—Leviticus 19:26

Mary Baker Eddy (1821–1910), founder of Christian Science

authority to end suffering? Authorization to "pull the plug" or post the DNR (Do Not Resuscitate) notice is more frequently determined by the patient who provides a living will. The greatest controversy surrounds euthanasia, which translates literally as a "good" or "happy death."

Is passive euthanasia—ending life support or nutrition—murder? Is active euthanasia—helping a terminally ill patient die—murder and suicide? Suicide is not specifically condemned in the Bible. However, it is seen as murder (of oneself), a sin for which one logically cannot obtain forgiveness.

Discoveries in the field of genetic research bring another avalanche of ethical dilemmas. Amniocentesis, the process of withdrawing and analyzing fluids surrounding the fetus, can determine potential congenital disorders, such as Down's syndrome, causing some parents to debate the worth of carrying a fetus to full term. In the past, an imperfect infant was often seen as a punishment, but is now accepted as a whole person who provides an opportunity to express unconditional Christian love.

Historically, congenital and inherited diseases have also been looked on as punishment from God—"visiting the iniquity of the fathers upon the children, and upon the children's children, unto the third and to the fourth generation" (Exodus 34:7). This verse has also been used in reference to sexually transmitted disease. Only in recent years has Attention Deficit Disorder been diagnosed and medically treated. Are these chronically hyperactive, disobedient, and otherwise unruly children no longer simply "full of the Devil"?

Discoveries in genetic research may ultimately challenge the concepts of sin, guilt, and personal responsibility for one's actions. Researchers may be able to determine predispositions to mental illness, obesity, sexual orientation, a specific level of intelligence, criminal behavior, alcoholism—even left-handedness, which at one time was discouraged, considered to be abnormal, undesirable, and even evil.

Reverend Ted Peters, professor at Pacific Lutheran Theological Seminary in Berkeley, California, voiced a common concern: "As a society, we seem to believe that if our behavior is biologically determined, then the genes we inherit—not we ourselves—can be held responsible for what we do."

If, in fact, a genetic correlation can be found, there is a danger of discrimination from birth if an indi-

The Bible Tells Me So

"Jesus Healing the Sick Man of the Palsy." Nineteenth-century engraving by Gustave Doré (Matthew 9:2–7).

vidual's current or inevitable future condition is known. Genetic technology could become a scientific tool for proving inferiority.

The Catholic Church opposes tests for fetal malformation and congenital disease because of the possibility of abortions, and mainstream Protestant and Jewish groups have adopted positions on this issue, some suggesting a halt to screening and prenatal testing until these ethical questions are answered.

Genetic research is used as a justification to condemn abortion—the distinct chromosomal profile of a fetus proves unique "personhood." And it influences the debate over the origin of the

And, behold, they brought to him a man sick of the palsy, lying on a bed: and Jesus seeing their faith said unto the sick of the palsy; Son, be of good cheer; thy sins be forgiven thee. And, behold, certain of the scribes said within themselves, This man blasphemeth. And Jesus knowing their thoughts said, Wherefore think ye evil in your hearts? For whether is easier, to say, Thy sins be forgiven thee; or to say, Arise, and walk? But that ye may know that the Son of man hath power on earth to forgive sins, (then saith he to the sick of the palsy,) Arise, take up thy bed, and go unto thine house. And he arose, and departed to his house. But when the multitudes saw it, they marvelled, and glorified God, which had given such power unto men.

—Matthew 9:2–8

And ye shall know the truth, and the truth shall make you free.

—John 8:32

It shall be a perpetual statute for your generations throughout all your dwellings, that ye eat neither fat nor blood.

—Leviticus 3:17

A Dominican nun dispensing medicine (1800s)

human race and the concept of evolution, revealing more similarities than differences in a comparison of humans with other creatures, such as chimpanzees, which brings up issues relevant to the ethical treatment of what many consider to be our close genetic relatives.

Many biblical dietary laws and the proscriptions against the abuse of alcohol have been scientifically proven as sound, and these guidelines have influenced behaviors in the daily lives of many, such as Seventh-Day Adventists and Mormons.

Faith healers have a long history of gaining converts and large bank accounts, duping the desperate and making their use of the Bible a point of satire and ridicule. But the cornerstone of many ministries has been the establishment of hospitals and medical centers. These religious groups and their medical staffs obviously don't feel that they are playing God. They are doing God's work. Jesus and his apostles were healers.

It is only in the past fifty years that medicine has become a science: cold, clinical, and calculating. The patient risks becoming an object, no longer a human being. We are now seeing a return to holistic medicine—treating the whole person—and increasing involvement and interest on the part of medical professionals with the role that prayer and spiritual life play in the healing process.

Procedures that have never been viewed as provoking religious controversy continue to appear. In Chicago, in 1994, a young mother-to-be was warned by her doctors that, unless delivered by cesarean, her baby would die or suffer severe brain damage. Deeply religious people, the woman and her husband wanted a natural birth and believed a miracle would occur to save the baby. They wanted no interference from doctors or child welfare authorities. The Illinois Supreme Court determined that the state could not force her to have a cesarean. Before any more legal steps could be taken, a healthy baby was born.

Arlington National Cemetery, Arlington, Virginia

Be merciful, O Lord, unto thy people Israel, whom thou hast redeemed, and lay not innocent blood unto thy people of Israel's charge. And the blood shall be forgiven them. So shalt thou put away the guilt of innocent blood from among you, when thou shalt do that which is right in the sight of the Lord.
—Deuteronomy 21:8–9

But love ye your enemies, and do good, and lend, hoping for nothing again; and your reward shall be great, and ye shall be the children of the Highest: for he is kind unto the unthankful and to the evil.
—Luke 6:35

The Lord is a man of war: the Lord is his name.
—Exodus 15:3

And the fruit of righteousness is sown in peace of them that make peace.
—James 3:18

To Oppose or Justify War

Lessons of warfare in the Bible range from heavenly sanctioned wars of conquest and God's punishment (see, for example, Numbers 31, the war against Midian) to Jesus' words and deeds of nonviolence. In the New Testament, war is fought on a spiritual plane, with the final battle to be fought at The End.

New Testament lessons of nonviolence were important to early Christians—and set them apart as the new "chosen people." Early church fathers interpreted Matthew 26:52 as a reason for soldiers to drop their weapons. Chris-

tians who refused to fight did a greater service by praying to rid the land of the demons who caused strife—war, but on a spiritual battlefield.

The army of the Roman Empire posed the problem of idolatry, not only because of the non-Christian religious practices of soldiers, but in terms of allegiance to a divine emperor. Some soldiers who refused to fight were martyred. Others deserted and were imprisoned.

By the time of the rule of Constantine, when Christianity was incorporated into the empire, the attitude toward war began to change. Early in the fifth century, only Christians could serve in the

"Both [sides] read the same Bible, and pray to the same God; and each invokes his aid against the other . . ."

—Abraham Lincoln, Second Inaugural Address on the Civil War (1865)

Science, Medicine, and the World

113

Thou shalt not kill.

—Exodus 20:13

And take the helmet of salvation, and the sword of the Spirit, which is the word of God.

—Ephesians 6:17

And if Satan cast out Satan, he is divided against himself; how shall then his kingdom stand?

—Matthew 12:26

For the Lord your God is he that goeth with you, to fight for you against your enemies, to save you.

—Deuteronomy 20:4

When a man hath taken a new wife, he shall not go out to war, neither shall he be charged with any business: but he shall be free at home one year, and shall cheer up his wife which he hath taken.

—Deuteronomy 24:5

"God wills it"—the battle cry of the Crusades.

"Remember that the German people are the chosen of God. On me, on me as German Emperor, the Spirit of God has descended. I am His weapon, His sword, and His vizard! Woe to the disobedient! Death to cowards and unbelievers!"

—Kaiser Wilhelm II, as quoted by David Lloyd George in an address of September 19, 1914

Roman army. There were contradictions, such as a decree that soldiers who had killed an enemy were to abstain from communion for three years. In the Middle Ages, some leaders advocated the use of the mace for clubbing their enemies to death in order to avoid "shedding blood." But war was unavoidable. Followers of the New Testament had to decide whether to fight and preserve home and freedom of worship, or to choose pacifism and risk being conquered and denied the right of Christian worship.

Between 413 to 427 A.D., Augustine of Hippo developed the concept of the "just war," a war that should be waged by a proper, rec-ognized authority against a recognizable evil. Christians could go to war on behalf of God, with peace as the objective. Priests and monks were excused from service.

It would be some time before the Tenth Commandment (concerning covetousness) would be brought into the argument against wars of conquest by "holy" empires. Christians were to battle heathens to reclaim the Holy Lands

"It is the object only of war that makes it honorable. And if there was ever a *just* war since the world began, it is this in which America is now engaged."

—Thomas Paine (1778)

*"Onward, Christian soldiers,
Marching as to war,
With the Cross of Jesus,
Going on before!"*

—**From a hymn by Sabine Baring-Gould (1864)**

in the name of the Cross, under the battle cry, "God wills it!"

The Augsburg Confession (1530) allowed Christians to serve as soldiers in just wars. John Calvin, bolstered by many passages of Scripture, determined that God deems war to be lawful: the Bible is rich with the use of images to encourage the "war" to spread the gospel with a militant missionary zeal (I Timothy 1:18). The correct way to interpret and live by the Scriptures provided excuses for wars between the devout and the "heretics," and between Protestants and Catholics, most recently in Northern Ireland.

In the New World, Christian nonviolence again came into play. English Quaker William Penn (1644–1718) founded a new colony that allowed Quakers to live without fear of religious persecution. They made peace with the natives, treated them fairly, and refused to fight. While violence surrounded their colony, Quakers enjoyed some thirty years of peace. They were finally joined by gun-carrying non-Quakers, who eventually made up the majority.

Science, Medicine, and the World

Native Americans weren't fooled, and the peace was ended.

Well into this century, Quakers and Mennonites have been the best organized Christian pacifists and conscientious objectors, focusing their service on relief and medical care in times of war.

Few will argue with the need, on June 6, 1944, to break Hitler's stranglehold on Europe. The debate still continues about the necessity of dropping atomic bombs on Japan, although these

"Thoughts on the Nature of War, and Its Repugnancy to the Christian Life" by William Law and Thomas Harley, featuring Luke 9:23 on the title page (London, 1766)

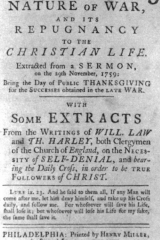

"I am not here to talk surrender terms, but to talk about how to fight and win the cultural war for the soul of our country . . . Our culture is superior because our religion is Christianity and that is the truth that makes men free."

—**Pat Buchanan speaking at the Christian Coalition's "Road to Victory" conference (1993)**

And he shall judge among the nations, and shall rebuke many people: and they shall beat their swords into plowshares, and their spears into pruninghooks: nation shall not lift up sword against nation, neither shall they learn war any more.

—**Isaiah 2:4**

Depart from evil, and do good; seek peace, and pursue it.

—**Psalm 34:14**

Then said Jesus unto him, Put up again thy sword into his place: for all they that take the sword shall perish with the sword.

—**Matthew 26:52**

Blessed are the peacemakers: for they shall be called the children of God.

—**Matthew 5:9**

> A time to love, and a time to hate; a time of war, and a time of peace.
>
> —Ecclesiastes 3:8

> Those things, which ye have both learned, and received, and heard, and seen in me, do: and the God of peace shall be with you.
>
> —Philippians 4:9

> This charge I commit unto thee, son Timothy, according to the prophecies which went before on thee, that thou by them mightest war a good warfare.
>
> —I Timothy 1:18

> Therefore to him that knoweth to do good, and doeth it not, to him it is sin.
>
> —James 4:17

Seventeenth-century engraving depicting the "angel of the Lord" in the camp of the Assyrians, who "smote . . . an hundred fourscore and five thousand" (II Kings 19:35)

DENOMINATIONS REFUSING MILITARY SERVICE:

Brethren in Christ (also referred to as the River Brethren or the Church of the Brethren)

Mennonites

Quakers, or Society of Friends

Jehovah's Witnesses

---

actions did bring the war to an end.

During the Vietnam era, Christian anti-war activists and draft resisters followed their convictions while President Richard Nixon sought guidance from Billy Graham. President George Bush wanted to ensure that, in the case of Operation Desert Storm in the Persian Gulf, it would be a "good war" from a Christian perspective. Southern Baptist Air Force chaplain Reverend Garland Robertson was disciplined and forced to retire because he publicly criticized that war. The definition of Augustine's "just war" looks very similar to the policy now in place in the post–Cold War era, as military and political leaders ponder entry into some hot spot on the globe, weighing peacekeeping against peacemaking.

At two A.M. on Pearl Harbor Day, 1993, four Catholic peace activists walked undetected into an Air Force base in North Carolina and attacked an F-15 fighter bomber plane with hammers. They did succeed in doing some damage before being arrested, and claimed to be ". . . prayerfully beginning the process of nonviolent disarmament . . . we're just at the beginning of a peace movement." The judge who sentenced them called them "dangers to the community."

The interpretation of Christ's message will always be at odds with the convictions of our leaders, popular opinion, and the individual who is asked to lift up the sword.

In 1995, the American Militia movement came to light. Merging biblical and constitutional fundamentalism, its members banded together to fight a government they see as "Godless."

> "North Carolina militia leader Albert Esposito urged his group . . . to stock up immediately on the 'Four B's: Bibles, bullets, beans, and bandages . . . to resist the coming New World Order.' "
>
> —From a news story reported one month after the bombing of a federal building in Oklahoma City (1995)

To Prove That the Earth Is the Center of the Universe

A young mathematics professor in Italy, Galileo Galilei, was required to teach a course in astronomy based on a centuries-old theory that the sun and planets revolved around the Earth. The theory, which held that the Earth is the center of the universe, provided "scientific" proof of the biblical concept.

Over time, Galileo became convinced of the accuracy of heliocentrism, proposed by Polish astronomer Nicolaus Copernicus (1473–1543): all planets, including the Earth, revolve around the sun. Copernicus—himself a church official—had treated heliocentrism as theory rather than to reveal his belief that it was the true state of the universe. This kept him out of trouble with the church. Galileo would be much more candid.

Albrecht Dürer engraving "The Eastern Hemisphere Celestial Globe" (1515), based on the world as known in the time of Ptolemy, with some updates.

In 1613, Galileo wrote a letter in which he tried to show that the Copernican theory was consistent with both Catholic doctrine and proper biblical interpretation. The letter fell into the hands of some of his enemies, who sent a copy to the Inquisitors in Rome. He was cleared, but ordered not to "hold or defend" the Copernican theory.

"There is no doubt that Galileo was prosecuted by the Roman inquisition . . . who endeavored to make a Church tribunal the judge of scientific truth, a function . . . which it was not competent to exercise . . ."

—James J. Walsh, K.C. St. G., M.D., Ph.D., Litt.D., L.L.D.; Dean, Fordham University School of Medicine; Professor of Physiological Psychology, Cathedral College, New York (1911)

Their line is gone out through all the earth, and their words to the end of the world. In them hath he set a tabernacle for the sun.
—Psalm 19:4

Hast thou with him spread out the sky, which is strong, and as a molten looking glass?
—Job 37:18

And God made the firmament, and divided the waters which were under the firmament from the waters which were above the firmament: and it was so.
—Genesis 1:7

The mighty God, even the Lord, hath spoken, and called the earth from the rising of the sun unto the going down thereof.
—Psalm 50:1

And after these things I saw four angels standing on the four corners of the earth, holding the four winds of the earth, that the wind should not blow on the earth, nor on the sea, nor on any tree.
—Revelation 7:1

And as soon as we had heard these things, our hearts did melt, neither did there remain any more courage in any man, because of you: for the Lord your God, he is God in heaven above, and the earth beneath.

—Joshua 2:11

The sun also ariseth, and the sun goeth down, and hasteth to his place where he arose.

—Ecclesiastes 1:5

Galileo Galilei, 1564–1642

In his defense, Galileo stated that interpreting Scripture as allegory had always been permitted. The problem lay in the fact that his interpretation differed from the official interpretation of the church.

In 1632, he published *Dialogue Concerning the Two Chief World Systems,* comparing the Ptolemaic-Aristotelian theory with Copernican theory to show that the latter was superior. The book uses the literary device of three people in conversation, and Galileo attacks arguments stated by Simplicio (translated as "fool"), who, as it turns out, speaks official church arguments.

Again summoned to Rome, Galileo was tried on "vehement suspicion of heresy" and forced to swear that he "abjured, cursed and detested" the errors of his work. He was found guilty and sentenced to life imprisonment in 1633. Because of his age, Galileo

Galileo argued for nonliteral interpretations of Joshua 10 (the scene depicted here in a seventeenth-century engraving) and Psalm 19. Earlier, Job 26 had been used by an ally of Copernicus to defend his theory.

was allowed to serve his imprisonment under house arrest. Despite blindness and ill health, he completed *Discourse on Two New Sciences,* published in 1638.

"They have endeavoured to spread the opinion that such [Copernican] propositions in general are contrary to the Bible and are consequently damnable and heretical . . . in purely physical matters, where faith is not involved, they would have us altogether abandon reason and the evidence of our senses in favour of some biblical passage, though beneath the surface meaning of its words this passage may contain a different sense."

—In Galileo's "Letter to Christina" (1615) from Stillman Drake's *Discoveries and Opinions of Galileo* as cited in his *Galileo* (1980)

In 1992—359 years after his conviction—The Vatican Commission of Historic, Scientific and Theological Inquiry (started in 1979) delivered a "not guilty" verdict. Galileo's judges were excused, forgiven because they couldn't understand a nonliteral reading of Scripture.

The trial of Galileo should not be viewed simply as a church versus science issue: while Galileo was a target of Jesuits, he enjoyed the support of others in the church hierarchy. The fear was that Galileo's theories would challenge Catholic tradition on a scientific front at the time when the church was fending off assaults from Reformation movements led by Luther and Calvin.

Galileo's *Dialogue Concerning Two Chief World Systems* remained in the official Index of Prohibited Books until 1835.

"Clarifications furnished by recent historical studies enable us to state that this sad misunderstanding now belongs to the past."

—**Pope John Paul II in 1992 on the occasion of declaring Galileo "rehabilitated." Galileo's case, he said, had become "the symbol of the church's supposed rejection of scientific progress."**

The Earth, as presented in an 1890 graphic

"Ptolomaeus Aegyptius" as depicted by Dürer in an engraving of the celestial globe (circa 1515)

Science, Medicine, and the World

He stretcheth out the north over the empty place, and hangeth the earth upon nothing.

—**Job 26:7**

And God said, Let there be lights in the firmament of the heaven to divide the day from the night; and let them be for signs, and for seasons, and for days and years: And let them be for lights in the firmament of the heaven to give light upon the earth: and it was so. And God made two great lights; the greater light to rule the day, and the lesser light to rule the night: he made the stars also. And God set them in the firmament of the heaven to give light upon the earth.

—**Genesis 1:14–17**

"Let there be light." Illustration for Milton's poems by John Martin (1860)

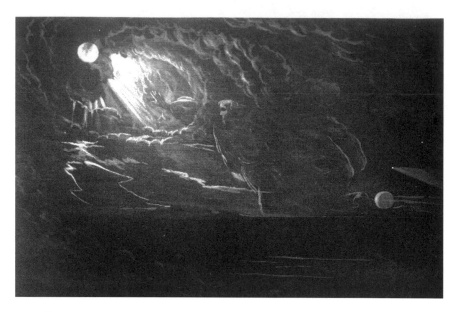

In the beginning God created the heaven and the earth. And the earth was without form, and void; and darkness was upon the face of the deep. And the Spirit of God moved upon the face of the waters. And God said, Let there be light: and there was light.

—Genesis 1:1–3

And on the seventh day God ended his work which he had made; and he rested on the seventh day from all his work which he had made.

—Genesis 2:2

For a thousand years in thy sight are but as yesterday when it is past, and as a watch in the night.

—Psalm 90:4

To Prove That God Created Man and the Universe

In July 1925, high school biology teacher John Scopes was found guilty of teaching evolution in violation of state law.

The Scopes "Monkey Trial" became a media spectacle, focusing America's attention on a dramatic, often humorous showdown between two legal titans: Clarence Darrow defending the biology teacher, and William Jennings Bryan heading the prosecution. Literally, the case banned the teaching of the theory of evolution in Tennessee public schools.

But to many, the trial showed a victory of the Bible over an atheistic, scientific theory that challenged it. The case seemed to show that the government of the state of Tennessee officially proved that evolution theory was flawed and that God created the heavens and the Earth in a manner strictly according to the biblical account. Efforts immediately began to enact similar laws in other states.

Over the next few decades, scientific evidence of dinosaurs became part of popular culture, in spite of its directly contradicting Genesis. Fossilized dinosaur remains began to populate museums around the world. Magazines and newspapers delivered vivid accounts of the finds of paleontologists, and television brought news of more discoveries into our living rooms and classrooms. The National Museum of Natural History annually hosts thousands of visiting schoolchildren, who marvel at a time line of Earth history extending millions and millions of years.

In 1968, laws dating from the Scopes era that made the teaching of evolution illegal in Tennessee, Mississippi, and Arkansas were declared unconstitutional. But a new scientific theory had taken root. Scientific Creationism's "young Earth" theory holds that the entire history of the planet has taken place in the past six thousand to ten thousand years. God created the world out of nothing in six twenty-four-hour days.

As early as the seventeenth century, complex formulas were devised to translate the biblical account of the time of creation into terms of modern timekeeping. James Ussher of Dublin determined in 1650 that God created the world on Saturday evening, October 22, 4004 B.C. John Light-

foot of Cambridge concluded in 1644 that Adam's creation occurred early in the morning of the autumn equinox in 3928 B.C. Different versions of Scriptures drew different conclusions, but an age of six thousand years became the most widely accepted.

Creationism relies heavily on the story of the Great Flood and its effect on the Earth's geology and animal life, and many biblical scholars focus on the feasibility of Noah's ark. Jesuit geologist Athanasius Kircher (1602–1680) calculated the ark's size, number of compartments, and necessary provisions for all 130 then-known species of mammals, 150 birds, and 30 reptiles.

Creationism is presented as a science that independently corroborates the Bible, contradicting prevailing and accepted scientific evidence of the Earth's age and the theories of its origin. Scientific Creationists ridicule evolutionary theory's randomness, its lack of purpose or design.

The Institute for Creation

"Darwinism not only robs us of revelation, but *removes the very foundation from under the whole structure of natural religion. . . .*"

—From an unsigned commentary against Darwinism, *Scribner's Monthly,* July 1875

And the Lord God formed man of the dust of the ground, and breathed into his nostrils the breath of life; and man became a living soul.
—Genesis 2:7

And the Lord God caused a deep sleep to fall upon Adam, and he slept: and he took one of his ribs, and closed up the flesh instead thereof; And the rib, which the Lord God had taken from man, made he a woman, and brought her unto the man.
—Genesis 2:21–22

"Everywhere we have found a Divine Hand shaping and moulding to accomplish a Divine ideal. . . . Science and religion alike are His offspring. Both will ultimately vindicate Him and His attributes . . . and God shall be proclaimed LORD OF ALL!"

—Conclusion of a geology textbook by J. Dorman Steele, Ph.D., *The Story of the Rocks: Fourteen Weeks in Popular Geology* (1877)

And the flood was forty days upon the earth; and the waters increased, and bare up the ark, and it was lift up above the earth. And the waters prevailed, and were increased greatly upon the earth; and the ark went upon the face of the waters. And the waters prevailed exceedingly upon the earth; and all the high hills, that were under the whole heaven, were covered.

—Genesis 7:17–19

"Le monde primitif." Woodcut of dinosaurs based on fossil evidence, Paris. (1857)

"You cannot in academic honesty say that 'I am a Christian,' and that 'I am a believer in God' and [at the same time say] 'I accept evolution.' "

—Televangelist Jerry Falwell (1985)

Research requires adherents to sign a statement of faith that the biblical account of Creation is "true and scientifically accurate."

In 1987, the United States Supreme Court, in the case of *Edwards* v. *Aguillard,* ruled that teaching the biblical account of creation may violate the constitutional guarantee of separation of church and state. Creationists argue that suppression of their viewpoint prevents true debate about evolutionary theory. But others can argue that Creationism as scientific support of biblical literalism is as blasphemous as the theory it purports to refute. By incorporating the language of the enemy (science), it reduces the words of the Bible to yet another scientific theory.

Only in Sunday schools and church-funded schools can students learn that perhaps the dinosaurs were actually the Old Testament monsters, Leviathan (Job

"[Barney the dinosaur is] straight out of the new age and the world of demons and devils . . . Barney is teaching kids that we must accept everyone as they are—whether they're homosexuals or lesbians."

—Reverend Joseph Chambers, radio evangelist (1993)

The Bible Tells Me So

"Mr. Darwin tells us that Evolution proceeds by 'numerous, successive, and slight modifications.' Paul knew that, and put it, only in more beautiful words, . . . 'The inward man . . . is renewed from day to day.' "

—Henry Drummond (1851–1897), Scottish writer and evangelist, *The Greatest Thing in the World*

41:1; Isaiah 27:1; Psalm 104:26) and Behemoth (Job 40:15-24); that skulls of prehistoric men are more likely the disfigured remains of lepers; and that dinosaur bones were planted by Satan to test our faith, a theory put forth over a century ago.

Meanwhile, Barney the purple dinosaur danced into the lives of millions of toddlers, *Jurassic Park* broke box-office records around the world, and fossil discoveries established a "family tree" of the human race going back to an ancestor in Ethiopia six million years ago.

In *Genesis and the Big Bang: The Discovery of Harmony Between Modern Science and the Bible,* Gerald L. Schroeder, Ph.D., proposes that the Bible and science are not contradictory after all. The evolution over billions of years following the "big bang" and the first six days that begin Genesis are actually the same event, told at different points in history and in a different language, based on mankind's ability to understand. He writes: "Theological arguments based on faulty understanding of either natural science or the Bible are counterproductive to a search for truth in any age and especially during an age that puts so much credence in science."

"True science to an ever-increasing degree discovers God as though God were waiting behind each closed door opened by science."

—Pope Pius XII (1951)

O Timothy, keep that which is committed to thy trust, avoiding profane and vain babblings, and oppositions of science falsely so called: Which some professing have erred concerning the faith. Grace be with thee. Amen.

—I Timothy 6:20–21

Science, Medicine, and the World

124

But ask now the beasts, and they shall teach thee; and the fowls of the air, and they shall tell thee: Or speak to the earth, and it shall teach thee; and the fishes of the sea shall declare unto thee. Who knoweth not in all these that the hand of the Lord hath wrought this? In whose hand is the soul of every living thing, and the breath of all mankind.

—Job 12:7–10

And God said, Let us make man in our image, after our likeness: and let them have dominion over the fish of the sea, and over the fowl of the air, and over the cattle, and over all the earth, and over every creeping thing that creepeth upon the earth.

—Genesis 1:26

Pesticides and chemical fertilizers, in use for decades, eliminate the need for a "rest" for the land.

To Exploit or Save the Environment

The Bible commands that man "have dominion . . . over all the earth, and over every creeping thing that creepeth upon the earth" (Genesis 1:26) and "subdue it: and have dominion over . . . every living thing that moveth upon the earth" (Genesis 1:28). Few living things—and their habitats—have not been subdued, changed, and in many cases destroyed in the name of human need.

For many, the Bible encourages a short-term perspective. The "final days" are upon us. Shouldn't we be more concerned with the afterlife than this planet, where we make only a brief stopover on the way to heaven?

At the end of the twentieth century, there is finally an awareness of the environmental crises facing our planet. Many Christians are beginning to make this issue an important part of their faith as well as their actions.

Individual congregations have taken on projects in their own communities. In a national conference, black churches resolved to

"In the good old puritan tradition we have taken the book of Genesis seriously and set out to subdue the Earth, and to have dominion over all things. And in two hundred years we have subdued it with asphalt, DDT, and industrial waste. But some of our leaders seem to think that it is the will of God, and if you tend not to believe it, then you can check the GNP."

—Reverend Channing E. Phillips, Washington, D.C., April 22, 1970, as quoted from "Unity" in *Earth Day—The Beginning: A Guide for Survival* (1970)

And God blessed them, and God said unto them, Be fruitful, and multiply, and replenish the earth, and subdue it: and have dominion over the fish of the sea, and over the fowl of the air, and over every living thing . . .

—Genesis 1:28

become players in the development of environmental policy, noting that many of their communities are threatened by toxic and hazardous waste sites. Sister Miriam Therese MacGillis, author and director of Genesis Farm, a gardening project supported by the community in northern New Jersey, asks, "why should we build more Catholic hospitals to care for the sick while we ignore the pollution of the land, water and air in our community that contributes to sickness?"

Many congregations have been independently sharing the Scriptural inspiration that can lead the faithful to environmental awareness. A national turning point came with the celebration of Earth Day, 1994. With study guides tailored for Protestant, Catholic, and Jewish congregations, the Environmental and Economic Justice/Hunger Concerns Working Group of the National Council of Churches of Christ in the USA published *God's Earth, Our Home: A Resource for Congregational Study and Action on Environmental and Economic Justice,* a strategy to bring people of faith together as a powerful force in the environmental movement. The work makes a strong case for environmental responsibility using Scriptures from the Old and New Testaments.

In a suggested service of worship, the "Call to Confession" acknowledged humankind's collective guilt for exploiting and destroying the Earth. In the "Prayer of Confession," the congregation admitted to God that "We have not loved the earth as you love it." In gratitude to Native Americans for their belief in the sanctity of the earth, their prayers are included, with references to "Mother Earth" and "The Great Spirit." And the Scriptures were called into service.

Christian stewardship is con-

"Indians Viewing the Improvements of White Men," from an 1847 geography textbook

> Speak unto the children of Israel, and say unto them, When ye come into the land which I give you, then shall the land keep a sabbath unto the Lord. Six years thou shalt sow thy field, and six years thou shalt prune thy vineyard, and gather in the fruit thereof; But in the seventh year shall be a sabbath of rest unto the land, a sabbath for the Lord: thou shalt neither sow thy field, nor prune thy vineyard. That which groweth of its own accord of thy harvest thou shalt not reap, neither gather the grapes of thy vine undressed: for it is a year of rest unto the land.
> —Leviticus 25:2–5

nected to stewardship of the Earth. "Dominion" no longer means exploitation. Harmony of the planet works side-by-side with harmony of the soul, and environmental consciousness can become a part of personal habits and personal politics.

In the fight to repair and preserve the environment, the Bible can be used to confirm a sacred contract between God and man. Each believer can make sure that the Earth is accorded the respect and love that comes from its creator.

All the faithful, regardless of denomination, can work together to leave a healthy planet to future generations until the inevitable return of Christ.

> " . . . we hear God calling our churches to care more intentionally for all of creation . . . therefore, be it resolved that each local church be encouraged to celebrate Earth Day . . . living in an economically and ecologically sound way that preserves the future of life on the planet."
> —Excerpt from the resolution in preparation for Earth Day 1995, General Board of Church and Society, the United Methodist Church

The Bible Tells Me So

To Predict the Time of the End of the World

Concern with the "final days" is an important part of many Christians' lives, particularly those who read the Bible literally. For some, it is the cornerstone of their faith.

There have been many "final days." William Miller (1782–1849) predicted The End would come in 1843. Then in 1844. Some of his followers designated a specific day—October 22. His publication, *The Midnight Cry,* featured both symbolic and literal illustrations of the events and beasts, dragons and other monsters that would be encountered. On the morning of October 23, 1843, an estimated fifty thousand people, many having disposed of their earthly possessions, some reportedly in white robes, were participants in what became known as The Great Disappointment.

For others it is an obsession, almost a sub-religion, a point of fascination, and a reality where biblical prophecy and ominous worldwide events converge to make it appear that the "time is right." Hurricanes, wars, earthquakes, famine, scientific and technological advances, diseases, the atomic bomb, the founding of Israel, the election of a Catholic president (Kennedy), the Cher-

Road sign in Green County, Georgia (June 1941)

nobyl nuclear accident ("Chernobyl" translates as "wormwood," number three of seven trumpets that will sound during the tribulation), and Mikhail Gorbachev's birthmark (the mark of the Beast?) have all been claimed "signs of the times."

Terms associated with the end have become part of everyday language. The best known include the tribulation (Mark 13:24); the last great battle, at a place called Armageddon (Revelation 16:14–16); the millennium—the thousand-year reign of Christ after the Second Coming (Revelation 20:2 and Revelation 20:6); the Rapture (I Thessalonians 4:17, Revelation 1:7); the Antichrists (Matthew 24:24 and I John 2:18), and the Four Horsemen of the Apocalypse (Revelation 6:1–10). Other books of the Bible

Take ye heed, watch and pray: for ye know not when the time is.
—Mark 13:33

Verily I say unto you, This generation shall not pass, till all these things be fulfilled.
—Matthew 24:34

Here is wisdom. Let him that hath understanding count the number of the beast: for it is the number of a man; and his number is Six hundred threescore and six.
—Revelation 13:18

The Rapture, from a seventeenth-century engraving

And the gospel must first be published among all nations.

—Mark 13:10

But in those days, after that tribulation, the sun shall be darkened, and the moon shall not give her light.

—Mark 13:24

Blessed and holy is he that hath part in the first resurrection: on such the second death hath no power, but they shall be priests of God and of Christ, and shall reign with him a thousand years.

—Revelation 20:6

Title page of "The Day of Doom" by Reverend Michael Wigglesworth (1662)

Highway sign between Columbus and Augusta, Georgia (1940)

WAR BRINGS DEATH O AMERICA! PREPARE FOR ETERNITY "PREPARE TO MEET GOD"

are used, including Ezekiel and Daniel.

The "number of the beast" is 666 (Revelation 13:18). Some question its significance. Others put great emphasis on it. Scholars point out that in Hebrew and Greek, names can be calculated to have a numerical value. "666" is purportedly the numerical value of "Nero Caesar" in Hebrew, as well as "Vicarius Filii Dei" in Latin. (It translates to "Vicar of Jesus Christ," presumably in reference to the pope.)

Ronald Reagan had the street numbers of his California retire-ment home resequenced to avoid the number "666" in his new address.

For some religious leaders, the end is the primary focus of their ministries and fund-raising. The more serious have shed themselves of all their material possessions, settled debts, and put any remaining money into the expenses incurred while awaiting the final days and the Rapture.

Cult leader David Koresh of Waco, Texas, was obsessed with the seventh seal, as shown in Revelation. With his compound surrounded by federal agents, he was present at his own Armageddon as he and his followers burned.

Some have been accused of using the impending doomsday as a political tool. In the '80s, many popular books on the subject appeared on the market, such as Hal Lindsey's *The Late Great Planet Earth* (1970), which sold 28 million copies by 1990. Lindsey's *The 1980s: Countdown to Armageddon* (1980) stayed on *The New York Times* best-seller list for over twenty weeks.

Concern arose that the message of the final days could have political ramifications. Some politicians could justify their objectives through preparing the world for this inevitability, and give Christian conservatives a reason for even more political involvement. If

"Everything is falling into place. It can't be too long now. Ezekiel says that fire and brimstone will be rained upon the enemies of God's people. That must mean they'll be destroyed by nuclear weapons . . . Gog, the nation that will lead all of the other powers of darkness against Israel, will come out of the north . . . Gog must be Russia . . . now that Russia has set itself against God . . . it fits the description of Gog perfectly."

—Future President Ronald Reagan, in a speech delivered during a political function (1971)

The Seventh-Day Adventist Church, founded in large part on the theory that Christ would return in the mid-1800s, issued an official statement opposing the prediction of specific dates for the Second Coming. (1995)

political and military leaders and policy makers shared this belief, the repercussions could be immense regarding the nuclear arms build-up, economic policies, treaty negotiations, relations with other countries (specifically Israel), and environmentalism. The belief in a finite future would inevitably affect decision-making and any long-term planning. The atomic bomb could provide a self-fulfilling prophecy.

Most Christian Americans can probably recall the childhood terror of a sermon warning of a specific or impending date for Armageddon. It's also a proven technique to gain converts. So far, most have been disappointed.

In 1971, Herbert W. Armstrong, chairman of the Worldwide Church of God, predicted a series of Apocalyptic events. After they failed to materialize, he stated that "Moses made mistakes, Abraham made mistakes, David made mistakes, Elijah made mistakes, Peter made mistakes, and so have all men God has ever called and used."

For most Christians, preoccupation with the end is not a part of day-to-day Christian living.

After all, Jesus himself said, "Take ye heed, watch and pray: for ye know not when the time is" (Mark 13:33).

For they are the spirits of devils, working miracles, which go forth unto the kings of the earth and of the whole world, to gather them to the battle of that great day of God Almighty. Behold, I come as a thief. Blessed is he that watcheth, and keepeth his garments, lest he walk naked, and they see his shame. And he gathered them together into a place called in the Hebrew tongue Armageddon.
—Revelation 16:14–16

And he laid hold on the dragon, that old serpent, which is the Devil, and Satan, and bound him a thousand years.
—Revelation 20:2

The Beast of Revelation, from a seventeenth-century Bible

Science, Medicine, and the World

Then we which are alive and remain shall be caught up together with them in the clouds to meet the Lord in the air: and so shall we ever be with the Lord.

—I Thessalonians 4:17

Behold, he cometh with clouds; and every eye shall see him, and they also which pierced him: and all kindreds of the earth shall wail because of him. Even so, Amen.

—Revelation 1:7

For there shall arise false Christs, and false prophets, and shall shew great signs and wonders; insomuch that, if it were possible, they shall deceive the very elect.

—Matthew 24:24

Little children, it is the last time: and as ye have heard that antichrist shall come, even now are there many antichrists; whereby we know that it is the last time.

—I John 2:18

"The Four Horsemen of the Apocalypse" by Albrecht Dürer

Notes

To Justify Slavery

The Scriptural arguments for slavery are most evident in the rebuttals from the North, and two excellent resources are the Reverend Gilbert Haven's *Sermons, Speeches and Letters on Slavery and Its War* (Lee and Shepard, Boston: 1869) and the politically explosive *Compendium of the Impending Crisis of the South* (A. B. Burdick, New York: 1860) by Hinton Rowan Helper, which was primarily an economic argument against slavery. In *Slavery Defended: The Views of the Old South* (Prentice-Hall, Englewood Cliffs, New Jersey: 1963), Eric L. McKitrick presents an excellent overview of period essays and writings (in which Stringfellow and Calhoun are cited), 8-9, 11, 94. Also valuable are William J. Cooper, Jr.'s *Liberty and Slavery: Southern Politics to 1860* (Alfred A. Knopf, New York: 1983); Kenneth M. Stampp's *The Peculiar Institution: Slavery in the Ante-Bellum South* (Vintage Books, New York: 1956); Forrest G. Wood's *The Arrogance of Faith: Christianity and Race in America from the Colonial Era to the Twentieth Century* (Alfred A. Knopf, New York: 1990); and W. O. Blake's *The History of Slavery and the Slave Trade; Ancient and Modern . . . The African Slave Trade and the Political History of Slavery in the United States* (J&H Miller, Columbus, Ohio: 1857), also as reprinted in 1971 by Negro History Press, Detroit, pp. 370 and 373, 377-378. For the story of the 1844-45 Baptist General Convention, see Henry C. Vedder's *A Short History of the Baptists* (The American Baptist Publication Society, Philadelphia, 1907) pp. 344-349. Frederick Douglass is quoted from his autobiography, *Narrative of the Life of Frederick Douglass, An American Slave, Written by Himself* (as reprinted by Signet Books from New American Library: 1968), p. 87.

To Justify the Abolishment of Slavery

In addition to the writings of Haven *(Sermons, Speeches, and Letters)* and Helper *(Compendium)*, also see period works such as *The Liberty Bell by the Friends of Freedom* (American Anti-Slavery Society, Boston: 1839), which included the essays by Garrison and Bradburn, and Charles K. Whipple's *Relations of Anti-Slavery to Religion* (Anti-Slavery Tracts, No. 19, American Anti-Slavery Society, New York: c. 1856). The abovementioned works on slavery also deal extensively with the abolitionist movement and arguments. Herbert Aptheker's *The Negro in the Abolitionist Movement* (International Publishers, New York: 1941) provides a valuable African-American perspective on the movement, and includes the quotation by Tornwell. The quotation from the article in *The Baltimore Sun* was cited by Helper. The anti-slavery hymn is from George W. Clark's *The Liberty Minstrel* (Saxon & Miles, New York, 1844).

To Justify the Superiority of White Protestants

For surveys of Klan history and discussions of rituals, see Richard K. Tucker's *The Dragon and the Cross: The Rise and Fall of the Ku Klux Klan in Middle America* (Archon Books: 1991); Larry R. Gerlach's *Blazing Crosses in Zion: The Ku Klux Klan in Utah* (Utah State University Press, Logan, Utah: 1982); William Loren Katz's *The Invisible Empire: The Ku Klux Klan Impact on History* (Open Hand Publishing, Inc., Seattle, WA: 1986); and David M. Chalmer's *Hooded Americanism: The History of the Ku Klux Klan* (Third Edition, Duke University Press, Durham, NC: 1987). An excellent collection of photographs depicting these rituals can be found in the Library of Congress, along with an extensive collection of Klan music from the 1920s.

To Prove a Black Presence in the Bible

In addition to the provocative discussions filling the media and many sermons and lectures dealing with this subject, one of the many excellent overviews is found in Cain Hope Felder's *Troubling Biblical Waters: Race, Class,* and Family (Orbis Books, Maryknoll, NY: 1989), also quoted from p. 20. Also see works such as John L. Johnson's *The Black Biblical Heritage: Four Thousand Years of Black Biblical History* (Winston-Derek Publishers, Inc., Nashville, TN: 1991). John Romer's *Testament: The Bible and History* (Henry Holt and Company, New York: 1988) includes an intriguing discussion of the representations of the Bible in popular culture. Among the many who have joined in the debate with Afrocentric claims concerning history, see Robert Hughes's *Culture of Complaint: The Fraying of America* (Oxford University Press, New York: 1993). Archbishop Stallings was quoted in Laurie Goodstein's "Stallings Campaign Targets White Depictions of Jesus," *The Washington Post,* April 10, 1993, p. B1. Bishop Henry M. Turner's "God Is a Negro" is from John H. Bracey, August Meier, and Elliot Rudwick, eds., *Black Nationalism in America* (The Bobbs–Merrill Company, Inc. Indianapolis and New York: 1970), p. 154. The words of the Bible have been made more accessible to young African-Americans by P. K. McCary, "Interpreter," *The Black Bible Chronicles—Book One: From Genesis to the Promised Land* (African American Family Press, an imprint of Multi Media Communicators, Inc., New York: 1993), p. 119. Reverend Haven's 1854 sermon is excerpted from Haven, *Sermons, Speeches, and Letters.*

To Justify Civil Rights for African-Americans

For an excellent survey of the words of the era, see *The Eyes on the Prize Civil Rights Reader,* Clayborne Carson, David J. Garrow, Gerald Gill, Vincent Harding, Darlene Clark Hine, general editors (Penguin Books, New York: 1991). To review the words of Martin Luther King, Jr., see his *I Have a Dream,* forward by Reverend Bernice A. King (HarperSanFrancisco, HarperCollins, copyright 1963, 1993 by Coretta Scott King), and *The Martin Luther King, Jr., Companion,* selected by Coretta Scott King, with an introduction by Dexter Scott King (St. Martin's Press, New York: 1993). Also see Charles E. Silberman, *Crisis in Black*

and White (Random House, New York: 1964); Stephen L. Carter, *The Culture of Disbelief: How American Law and Politics Trivialize Religious Devotion* (Basic Books, A Division of HarperCollins, New York: 1993).

For gospel music, we referred to an early source (probably with some "revisions" of the lyrics and a somewhat patronizing yet sincere introduction): Marshall W. Taylor, D.D., introduction by F. C. Hoyt, *A Collection of Revival Hymns and Plantation Melodies* (Marshall W. Taylor and W. C. Echols, Publishers, Cincinnati, OH: 1882), p. 148.

To Persecute the Jews

General background histories include Arnold A. Rogow (editor), *The Jew in a Gentile World: An Anthology of Writings About Jews, by Non-Jews,* introduction by C. P. Snow, epilogue by Harold D. Lasswell (The Macmillan Company, New York: 1961), from which we cited the quotes by Martin Luther and Thomas Jefferson; Malcolm Hay's *Europe and the Jews: The Pressure of Christendom on the People of Israel for 1900 Years,* introduction by Thomas Sugrue (Academy Chicago Publishers, Chicago: 1950 by the Beacon Press); David Englander, editor, *The Jewish Enigma* (George Braziller, New York: 1992); Gavin I. Langmuir's *History, Religion and Antisemitism* (University of California Press, Berkeley, Los Angeles, Oxford: 1990). Also see Sander Gilman's *The Jew's Body* (Routledge, New York and London: 1991) and Robert Lacy's *Ford: The Men and the Machine* (Little, Brown and Company, Boston and Toronto: 1986). The story of the Inquisition is covered in detail in Cecil Roth's *A History of the Marranos* (The Jewish Publication Society of America, Philadelphia: 1932). The Lutheran Church draft document is discussed and quoted from Gustav Niebuhr, "Antisemitic Writings Face Repudiation," *The Washington Post,* October 17, 1993, p. A5. From the extensive press coverage of Holocaust deniers, see, for example, "Denying the Holocaust" by Laura Shapiro with Mark Miller and Marcus Mabry, *Newsweek,* December 20, 1993, p. 120; and "Holocaust of Mirrors" by Laurie Goodstein, *The Washington Post,* October 1, 1993, p. C1. *The Religious Right: The Assault on Tolerance and Pluralism in America,* Alan M. Schwartz, editor (Anti-Defamation League, New York: 1994) provided quotes from Billy McCormack (p. 5), Jimmy Swaggart (p. 73), and Pat Robertson (pp. 42–43). A source of much misinformation regarding Jews is *The Jewish Peril: Protocols of the Learned Elders of Zion* ("The Britons," London: 1920).

To Define the Traditional Role of Women

Background information and discussions concerning the role of women logically overlap into the subjects of marriage and ordination. See Elizabeth Cady Stanton (and revising committee), *The Woman's Bible,* European Publishing Company, New York, 1895 (as reprinted in *The Original Feminist Attack on the Bible,* introduction by Barbara Welter, Arno Press, New York: 1974), which is quoted here, and Stanton's *Eighty Years and More: Reminiscences 1815–1897,* introduction by Gail Parker (Schocken Books, New York: 1971, reprint). Also see George H. Tavard's *Woman in the Christian Tradition* (University of Notre Dame Press, Notre Dame: 1973); Edith Deen's *All of the Women of the Bible* (Harper & Row, New York: 1955); and Uta Ranke-Heinemann's *Eunuchs for the Kingdom of Heaven: Women, Sexuality and the Catholic Church,* translated by Peter Heinegg (Penguin Books, New York: 1991, reprinted by arrangement with Doubleday). For information on Thomas Jefferson's Bible, see *The Jefferson Bible: The Life and Morals of Jesus of Nazareth,* introduction by F. Forrester Church (Beacon Press, Boston: 1989). Information on ancient menstruation from Janice Delaney, Mary Jane Lupton, and Emily Toth's *The Curse: A Cultural History of Menstruation* (revised, expanded edition, University of Illinois Press, Urbana and Chicago: 1988). For an original perspective on the women's movement, see Elizabeth Cady Stanton's *Eighty Years and More: Reminiscences 1815–1897,* introduction

by Gail Parker (Schocken Books, New York: 1971). Phyllis Schlafly quoted from her book *The Power of the Positive Woman* (Jove Publications, Inc., New York:1978).

To Provide Sanctuary to Political Refugees

References to this history and use of Scriptures include refugee testimony, church declarations, sermons, lectures, and articles such as Richard L. Kenyon's "Continuing a tradition: Churches have provided sanctuary for ages," *Milwaukee Journal,* December 4, 1982. Ignatius Bau presents a detailed analysis in *This Ground Is Holy: Church Sanctuary and Central American Refugees* (Paulist Press: New York, Mahwah, NJ: 1985) for a history of the movement and references to more Scriptures. Along with the extensive media coverage of the period, see Ann Crittenden's *Sanctuary: A Story of American Conscience and the Law in Collision* (Weidenfeld & Nicholson, New York: 1988). The notes relating to the testimony of René Sanchez at All Souls Unitarian Church, Washington, D.C., are from October 6, 1985 (copy of translated testimony on file). Also refer to literature and publications relating to the current mission and activities of Refugee Voices: A Ministry With Uprooted Peoples in Washington, D.C. "1-800-LEV-1933" from Susan Bibler Coutin's *The Culture of Protest: Religious Activism and the U.S. Sanctuary Movement* (Westview Press, Boulder, CO: 1993). An excellent overview of the movement is available in Renny Golden and Michael McConnell's *Sanctuary: The New Underground Railroad* (Orbis Books, Maryknoll, NY: 1986).

To Empower and Liberate the Poor

The history of the liberation theology movement and examples of Scriptural applications to the poor are detailed in Gustavo Gutiérrez's *The Power of the Poor in History,* translated by Robert R. Barr (Orbis Books, Maryknoll, NY: 1983); Phillip Berryman's *Liberation Theology: The Essential Facts About the Revolutionary Movement in Latin America and Beyond* (I. B. Tauris & Co., Ltd., London: 1987); Leonardo Boff's *Church: Charism & Power: Liberation Theology and the Institutional Church,* translated by John W. Diercksmeier (Crossroad Publishing, New York: 1985); and Paul Gauthier's *Christ, The Church and the Poor* (The Newman Press, Westminster, MD: 1965). The Desmond Tutu quote was heard on National Public Radio's "Talk of the Nation," October 10, 1994. Also see Reverend Nathaniel West, D.D., *The Complete Analysis of the Holy Bible* (A. J. Johnson, Publisher, New York: 1869); and Gustavo Gutiérrez in *A Theology of Liberation: History, Politics and Salvation,* translated and edited by Sister Caridad Inda and John Eagleson (Orbis Books, Maryknoll New York: 1973, 1984. Originally published as *Teología de la liberación, Perspectivas,* Lima: 1971).

To Accuse and Execute Women as Witches

A detailed analysis of *The Witch's Hammer (Malleus Maleficarum)* is found in *A History of Medical Psychology* by Gregory Zilboorg, M.D., in collaboration with George W. Henry, M.D. (W. W. Norton & Co., Inc., New York: 1941). Also see E. J. Burford and Sandra Shulman's *Of Bridles and Burnings: The Punishment of Women* (St. Martin's Press, New York: 1992); Chadwick Hansen's *Witchcraft at Salem* (George Braziller, New York: 1969); Carol F. Karlsen's *The Devil in the Shape of a Woman: Witchcraft in Colonial New England* (W. W. Norton & Company, New York and London: 1987); Uta Ranke-Heinemann's *Eunuchs for the Kingdom of Heaven: Women, Sexuality and the Catholic Church,* translated by Peter Heinegg (Penguin Books: 1991. Reprinted by arrangement with Doubleday); and the classic by Montague Summers, *The History of Witchcraft & Demonology* (Castle Books, Secaucus, NJ: 1992); Pierre de Lancre was quoted on p. 63. The Pat Robertson quote appeared in the "Perspectives" column of *Newsweek* (September 7, 1992, p. 15). In interviews with Charlie Rose, Larry King, and William F. Buckley, Jr., Robertson shrugged off the letter as something written by his staff. He has stated that it is accurate, based on his staff's corroboration with "feminists" and their writings. The quotation by Pierre de Lancre is from his "L'Incredulité et Mescreance du Sortilège" of 1622, as quoted by Montague Summers in *The History of Witchcraft & Demonology* (Castle Books, Secaucus, NJ: 1992), p. 63.

To Support or Oppose the Ordination of Women

Earlier sources include Margaret Fell's *Women's Speaking . . .* (1666) and Elizabeth Cady Stanton (and revising committee), *The Woman's Bible,* European Publishing Company, New York: 1895 (as reprinted in *The Original Feminist Attack on the Bible,* introduction by Barbara Welter, Arno Press, New York: 1974), which is quoted here; revising committee member Die-trick's comment is from pp. 153-154. Also see George H. Tavard's *Woman in the Christian Tradition* (University of Notre Dame Press, Notre Dame: 1973); Edith Deen's *All of the Women of the Bible* (Harper & Row, New York: 1955); Uta Ranke-Heinemann's *Eunuchs for the Kingdom of Heaven: Women, Sexuality and the Catholic Church,* translated by Peter Heinegg (Penguin Books, New York: 1991. Reprinted by arrangement with Doubleday); and *Women Priests: A Catholic Commentary on the Vatican Declaration,* edited by Leonard Swidler and Arlene Swidler (Paulist Press, New York: 1977). Reverend Geoffrey Kirk was quoted in Crispain Balmer's article for Reuter, "Anglicans Set to Vote on Ordaining," *The Washington Post,* November 7, 1992, p. G11. Reverend Cheryl Jordan was quoted in Gustav Niebuhr's "From the Pulpit, a Focus on Women," *The Washington Post,* April 9, 1993, pp. A1, A16. Also see Richard N. Ostling's "The Second Reformation," *Time,* November 23, 1992, pp. 53-58; and the Reuter report "Pope Bans Female Priests 'Definitively,' " *The Washington Post,* May 31, 1994, p. A12. Pope John Paul II as quoted by Daniel Williams in Pope Apologizes for Discrimination Against Women," *The Washington Post,* July 11, 1995, pp. A1, A12.

To Support or Oppose the Marriage of Priests

The primary verses used against the marriage of priests are found as early as 1888 in *Why Should Priests Wed?* by "J.C." (A.E. Costello, New York), anonymously written in response to the rise of anti-Catholic sentiments. The author also condemns the sexual indiscretions of Protestant ministers and evangelists; the quote is from pp. 4–5. The contemporary debate can be followed in Father James Kavanaugh's *A Modern Priest Looks at His Outdated Church* (Trident Press, New York: 1967); Andrew M. Greeley's *Priests in the United States: Reflections on a Survey* (Doubleday & Company, Inc., Garden City, NY: 1972); and E. Schillebeeckx's *Celibacy,* translated by C. A. L. Jarrott (Sheed and Ward, New York: 1968). This subject is also thoroughly covered in Uta Ranke-Heinemann's *Eunuchs for the Kingdom of Heaven: Women, Sexuality and the Catholic Church,* translated by Peter Heinegg (Penguin Books, New York: 1991. Reprinted by arrangement with Doubleday); see p. 39 concerning Jerome translations. A former priest's historical research and arguments from a personal perspective can be found in Terrance Sweeney's *A Church Divided: The Vatican Versus American Catholics* (Prometheus Books, Buffalo, NY: 1992); see pp. 90–99 concerning effects of celibacy canons. Also see Kenneth L. Woodward's "Mixed Blessings," *Newsweek,* April 16, 1993, pp. 38–41; and Andrew Greeley's "A View from the Priesthood," *Newsweek,* April 16, 1993, p. 45.

To Define and Punish the Crime of Sodomy

". . . unless a man was involved, it wasn't cognizable as sex." Nan Hunter, professor, Brooklyn School of Law (as quoted by Lisa Mundy, "The Scarlet S: DC's Sodomy Law from Top to Bottom," *Washington City Paper,* February 26, 1993, p. 8. A number of theologians hold the view that residents of Sodom engaged in gang rape. See *Homosexuality: The Test Case for Christian Sexual Ethics,* James P. Hanigan (Paulist Press, New York/Mahwah, NJ: 1988). Chapter 2 of the book gives a good explanation of gang rape, especially as a form of punishment. For more discussion of sodomy, see Lou Chibbaro, Jr., "Sodomy Law Repealed," *The Washington Blade,* September 17, 1993. Lou Chibbaro, Jr., "Jury 'Nullifies' sodomy charge against Gay men," *The Washington Blade,* August 27, 1993, p. 16; Ned Zeman, "The Whoopee Monster," a book report on Samuel S. Janus and Cynthia L. Janus's *The Janus Report on Sexual Behavior* (John Wiley & Sons, 1993), *Newsweek,* March 8, 1993; and Boyce Rensberger, "Sex Survey: What Men Do and How Often They Do It," *The Washington Post,* April 15, 1993, pp. A1, A16. Anyone who wants to get exhaustingly deep into the subject should read the collection of essays edited by Jonathan Goldberg, *Reclaiming Sodom* (Routledge, New York: 1994), which was a great help in many areas, particularly "Bowers v. Hardwick," pp. 117–142 (from State of Georgia court records) and Jonathan Ned Katz's essay, "The Age of Sodomitical Sin, 1607–1740," pp. 43–58. Verna Spayth is quoted from Joyce Murdoch, "Laws Against Sodomy Survive in 24 States," *The Washington Post,* April 11, 1993, p. A20.

To Prevent Masturbation

The definition of "onanism" provided by Richard H. Hutchings, M.D., in *A Psychiatric Work Book: A Lexicon of Terms Employed in Psychiatry and Psychoanalysis Designed for Students of Medicine and Nursing and Psychiatric Social Workers* (The State Hospitals Press, Utica, New York: 1939), p. 148. Victorian viewpoints on masturbation were found in *Religion and Medicine: The Moral Control of Nervous Disorders* (Moffat, Yard & Company, New York: 1908) by Elwood Worcester, D.D., PhD., Samuel McComb, M.A., D.D., and Isador H. Coriat, M.D.; also listed by Leigh Rutledge in *The Gay Book of Lists,* (Alyson Publications, Inc., Boston: 1987), pp. 74–76. General background on society's reaction to masturbation can be found in David Cole Gordon's *Self-Love* (Penguin Books, Baltimore, MD: 1968). Uta Ranke-Heinemann also deals with the subject in *Eunuchs for the Kingdom of Heaven: Women, Sexuality and the Catholic Church* (Penguin Books, New York: 1991.

Reprinted by arrangement with Doubleday). Ann Landers quote is from her column of November 21, 1993, as it appeared in *The Washington Post,* p. F7. One of the many religious publications available is the brochure, "What's Wrong with Masturbation" by Steve Gallagher (Pure Life Ministries, Crittenden, KY: 1993). Ancient Jewish law from Rachel Biale, *Women and Jewish Law: An Exploration of Women's Issues in Halakhic Sources* (Schocken Books, New York: 1984). Survey data (". . . most studies indicate that more than 90 percent of males and 60 percent of females masturbate at some point during their lives . . .") from *The Academic American Encyclopedia,* on-line edition (Grolier Electronic Publishing, Danbury, CT: 1993). Additional reference from Ned Zeman, "The Whoopee Monster," *Newsweek,* March 8, 1993, p. 56. See also "Mechanical Gathering of Sperm Called Moral," *National Catholic Reporter,* December 17, 1993, p. 10.

To Oppose Abortion

In addition to many sermons, televised discussions, rallies, and protests, and tracts on the subject, excellent sources are Randy Alcorn's *Pro Life Answers to Pro Choice Arguments,* foreword by Thomas A. Glessner (Multnomah Books: 1992); Craig Chilton's *The Pro-Choice Victory Handbook: Strategies for Keeping Your Abortion Rights* (B. Owl Publications, Evansdale, IA: 1992); and publications from the Religious Coalition for Reproductive Rights's *Educational Series* (Washington, DC: 1993), including Reverend George Luthringer, "Considering Abortion? Clarifying What You Believe"; Dr. Paul D. Simmons, "Personhood, the Bible, and the Abortion Debate" and "Religious Liberty: A Heritage at Stake"; Dr. John M. Swomley, "Abortion: A Christian Ethical Perspective"; and Dr. Roy Bowen Ward, "Is the Fetus a Person? The Bible's View." Also see articles by John T. Noonan, Jr., Judith Jarvis Thomson, and Mary Anne Warren in John Arras and Robert Hunt's *Ethical Perspectives in Modern Medicine* (Mayfield Publishing Company: 1983); Ben Graber, with Eileen K. W. Cudney, *Abortion: A Citizen's Guide to the Issues* (Alter Press, Coral Springs, FL: 1990);

and Ronald Reagan's *Abortion and the Conscience of the Nation,* afterwords by C. Everett Koop, M.D., and Malcolm Muggeridge (Thomas Nelson Publishers, Nashville, Camden, New York: 1984). The Randall Terry quote is from Alan M. Schwartz, editor, *The Religious Right* (New York: Anti-Defamation League: 1994), p. 113. The Don Treshman quote is from *Time,* August 30, 1993, p. 12. Trosch as quoted in Gustav Niebuhr "To Church's Dismay, Priest Talks of 'Justifiable Homicide' of Abortion Doctors," *New York Times,* August 24, 1994, p. A12. Margaret Sanger is quoted from the chapter "Contraceptives or Abortion?" in her book *Woman and the New Race* (Bretano's, New York: 1920), pp. 118-29. Cardinal John O'Connor as quoted in "Archbishop Contends Abortion Is Key Issue," *The New York Times,* June 25, 1984. p. D13.

To Justify Physical Punishment of Children

See Lois G. Forer's *Criminals and Victims: A Trial Judge Reflects on Crime and Punishment* (W. W. Norton & Company, New York: 1980) for an excellent overview of attitudes toward children in "The Child and the Law." Also see Irwin A. Hyman's (forward by Phil Donahue) *Reading, Writing, and the Hickory Stick: The Appalling Story of Physical and Psychological Abuse in American Schools* (Lexington Books, D. C. Heath and Company, Lexington, MA/Toronto: 1990), which also includes studies and surveys relating to the attitudes of specific religious groups. The Jonathan Edwards reference is from Charles Francis Potter's *The Story of Religion Told in the Lives of Its Leaders* (Garden City Publishing Company, Inc., Garden City, NY: 1929), p. 516. Martin Luther is quoted from his "We Must Often Try God's Patience" (1532, No. 1615) in *Luther's Works, Volume 54: Table Talk,* Theodore G. Tappert, editor and translator, and Helmut T. Lehmann, general editor (Fortress Press, Philadelphia: 1967), pp. 158-59. Samuel Butler is quoted from his *Hubridas,* Part II, of 1664.

To Regulate Clothing and Hairstyles

Good general references include Paul Tabori's *Secret and Forbidden: The Moral History of the Passions of Mankind* (A Signet Book from New American Library, Times Mirror, New York: 1966), from which the German priest is quoted, p. 164. Also see Lee Hall's *Common Threads: A Parade of American Clothing* (A Bullfinch Press Book, Little, Brown and Company, Boston: 1992) and Bernard Rudofsky's *The Unfashionable Human Body* (Doubleday & Company, New York: 1971). Wesley is quoted in Vincent L. Milner's *Religious Denominations of the World* (Bradley, Garretson & Co., Philadelphia: 1873). Also see Elizabeth Cady Stanton, *Eighty Years and More: Reminiscences 1815-1897,* introduction by Gail Parker (Reprint, Schocken Books, New York: 1971), p. 458.

Nineteenth-century lectures, sermons, and stories include Reverend T. DeWitt Talmage, D.D., in his *Social Dynamite; or the Wickedness of Modern Society* (Standard Publishing Company, Chicago: 1890) and *Caroline Jones; or, Outward and Inward Adorning* (American Reform Tract and Book Society, Cincinnati: 1860).

To Assign Guilt for Disease

For a good social history of both general disease and AIDS, see Susan Sontag, *Illness as Metaphor* and *AIDS and Its Metaphors,* published in one volume by Anchor Books/Doubleday (New York: 1990); Falwell quote ("AIDS is God's judgment . . ."), p. 149; Cotton Mather quote, p. 148. The government's response (and lack of it) to the AIDS crisis is detailed in the late Randy Shilts's *And the Band Played On: People, Politics and the AIDS Epidemic* (St. Martin's Press, New York: 1987); Shilts quotes Jerry Falwell extensively. Also see Dennis Altman's *AIDS in the Mind of America* (Anchor Press/Doubleday, New York: 1986). Harold Covington's writings are quoted in *Quarantines and Death: The Far Right's Homophobic Agenda,* a booklet published by the Center for Democratic Renewal, Atlanta, Georgia (1991) p. 29. The connection between religion and medicine shows up again in Jackson Lears's article, "The Prozac Society: Mental Health 'Miracles' in U.S. History," *The Washington Post,* December 5, 1993, p. C1. Also see "Findings Counter Theory on Syphilis" by Boyce Rensberger, *The Washington Post,* November 19, 1992, p. A10. Also see Vincent Young, "Christian Soldiers in AIDS Fight—Black Churches in DC Nourish Body and Soul," *The Washington Post,* February 20, 1993, p. D8. Quote referring to Native Americans ("God was angry . . .") from Alfred W. Crosby, "God . . . Would Destroy Them, and Give Their Country to Another People: The Mysterious Diseases that Nearly Wiped Out the Indians of New England Were the Work of the Christian God—Or So Both Pilgrims and Indians Believed" in *American Heritage* (American Heritage Publishing Company, Volume 29/Number 6: 1978) pp. 39-43. Cardinal John O'Connor quoted from a book he cowrote with Mayor Edward I. Koch, *His Eminence and Hizzoner: A Candid Exchange* (William Morrow and Company, Inc., New York: 1989) pp. 76 and 88.

To Argue the Inferiority of Black Peoples

The very complex background relating to the "Curse of Canaan" is discussed in depth in Thomas Virgil Peterson's *Ham and Japheth: The Mythic World of Whites in the Antebellum South,* forward by William A. Clebsch (ATLA Monograph Series, No. 12, The Scarecrow Press, Inc. and The American Theological Library Association, Metuchen, NJ, and London: 1978 L. Richard Bradley in "The Curse of Canaan and the American Negro," *Concordia Theological Monthly* (Concordia Publishing House, St. Louis, MO: 1971; Vol. 42: pp. 100-110); Alan Davies's *Infected Christianity: A Study of Modern Racism* (McGill-Queen's University Press, Kingston and Montreal: 1988); Forrest G. Wood's *The Arrogance of Faith: Christianity and Race in America from the Colonial Era to the Twentieth Century* (Alfred A. Knopf, New York: 1990); and Cain Hope Felder's *Troubling Biblical Waters: Race, Class, and Family* (Orbis Books, Maryknoll,

NY: 1989). Helper and Haven are from the sources cited above. Reverend King is quoted in *The Martin Luther King, Jr., Companion: Quotations from the Speeches, Essays, and Books of Martin Luther King, Jr.,* selected by Coretta Scott King, introduction by Dexter Scott King (St. Martin's Press, New York: 1993) in the section titled "Blacks and Whites." Concerning some of the early scientific arguments, see William Stanton's *The Leopard's Spots: Scientific Attitudes Toward Race in America* (The University of Chicago Press, Chicago: 1960). The booklet with Plecker's speech is *Eugenics in Relation to The New Family and the Law on Racial Integrity* (including a paper read before the American Public Health Association), issued by the Bureau of Vital Statistics, State Board of Health, Richmond, VA: 1924. Also see Carl F. H. Henry (consulting editor), Billy Graham (introduction), *The Biblical Expositor: The Living Theme of the Great Book with General and Introductory Essays and Exposition for Each Book of the Bible* (A. J. Holman Company, Division of J. B. Lippincott Company, Philadelphia and New York: 1960, 1973); Laurie Goodstein's "Jackson Offers No Apology for Blast at Christian Right," *The Washington Post,* December 9, 1994, p. A2; Phillis Wheatley's *Poems on Various Subjects, Religious and Moral,* as printed in London (1773); reprinted in facsimile in *The Collected Works of Phillis Wheatley,* edited by John C. Shields (Oxford University Press, New York: 1988), p. 18; an article ("We assert . . .") in the *Southern Literary Messenger,* 1858, as cited in Langston Hughes and Milton Meltzer's, *A Pictorial History of the Negro in America* (Crown Publishers, Inc., New York: 1968), p. 26. See also Reverend Gilbert Haven's *Sermons, Speeches and Letters on Slavery and Its War* (Lee and Shepard, Boston: 1869); and Richard J. Herrnstein and Charles Murray, *The Bell Curve* (Free Press, New York: 1994).

To Justify Discrimination, Intolerance, and Violence Toward Homosexuals

A very helpful source for this section was found in Randy Shilts's *And the Band Played On: People, Politics and the AIDS Epidemic* (St. Martin's Press, New York: 1987), which provided information not only on AIDS, but also on how anti-gay prejudice may have actually helped AIDS *become* an epidemic in the first place.

The Harold Covington quote ("God's greatest gift") is from his book *The March Upcountry* (1987) as quoted in the booklet *Quarantines and Death: The Far Right's Homophobic Agenda* (Center for Demo-cratic Renewal, Atlanta, GA: 1991), p. 13; this book also provided the Jerry Falwell quote ("brute beasts"), from his "Old Time Gospel Hour" television show, March 1984, p. 18. Reverend Pete Peters is quoted in the Gran Fury pamphlet, *The "Christian" Agenda Revealed* (1993). The Dixon quote is from Shilts, *And the Band Played On,* p. 322. The CBN quote is from the pamphlet *Gay Lib,* (Christian Broadcasting Network, Virginia Beach: 1990), p. 1; Grimstead ("vomit") is quoted in Chris Bull's "Why Bush Hates You," *The Advocate,* October 20, 1992, p. 43. The Catholic Catechism-related quotes are from Nick Bartolomeo's "Vatican Says Statement Doesn't 'Pass Judgement,' " *The Washington Blade,* July 31, 1992, p. 17. Also see Russell Cate's "New Catholic Catechism Urges 'Respect' for Gays," *The Washington Blade,* November 27, 1994, p. 27. More information can be obtained from John E. Yang's "Lines Drawn in Oregon Gay Rights Battle; Voters to Decide if Constitution Will Declare Homosexuality 'Abnormal, Wrong, Unnatural,' " *The Washington Post,* September 27, 1992, p. A21. Also see "Baptist Group Denounces Homosexuality," an Associated Press story appearing in *The Washington Post,* November 12, 1992, p. C6.

On the issue of discrimination and violence toward gays by religious fundamentalists, among others, see Bill Turque, Carolyn Friday, Jeanne Gordon, Daniel Glick, Katrin Snow, Peter Annin, Farai Chideya, Anthony Duignan-Cabrera, Patrick Rogers, Lynn Haessly, "Gays Under Fire," *Newsweek,* September 14, 1992, pp. 35–40; Colman McCarthy, "The Military's War Against Civil Liberties," *The Washington Post,* February 9, 1993, p. C11; Guy Trebay, "No Rest In Peace," *Voice,* March 8, 1994, p. 29; Kristina Campbell, "Gays Are Popular Target at Christian Coalition Meeting," *The Washington Blade,* September 17, 1993, p. 11; Knight-Ridder News Service, "Churches Spearheading Campaign to Restore Traditional Values," reported in *Asheville Citizen-Times,* June 27, 1992, p. 5B; and Associated Press, "Three Marines Charged in Assault on Gay Man," *The Washington Post,* February 2, 1993, p. A3. Anita Bryant as quoted in *Time* magazine's "Chronicles" section, "Maybe There's Something in the Juice," February 2, 1994, p.14.

For information on "ex-gay" ministries, see the documentary film *One Nation Under God* (1993) produced by Teodoro Maniaci and Francine M. Rzeznick (3Z/Hourglass Productions); also see Darice Clark, "Lecturer Discusses 'Causes' and 'Cures' of Homosexuality," *The Washington Blade,* October 1, 1993, p. 15. For a glimpse of reality not detailed in this story, see Cindy Loose, "Demonstrators Clash over Gay Rights," *The Washington Post,* April 14, 1994, p. D3, in which a man leaving Mass "aim[ed] his van" at a group of people he believed to be homosexual demonstrators: they were actually anti-homosexual demonstrators who then wanted to have him "charged with attempted murder. They changed their minds after [he] apologized, explaining that he had mistaken them for the homosexual group." And see how the churches and citizens of the picturesque tourist town of Asheville, North Carolina, reacted to a relatively small turnout for "Gay Pride Day" by staging a "family values day" called "March for the Family," featuring newspaper ads in the *Asheville Citizen-Times* headlined "Sin Sin Sin" (sic). See also the Knight-Ridder News Service story titled "Churches Spearheading Campaign to Restore Traditional Values," *Asheville Citizen-Times,* June 27, 1992, p. 5B, and "They Came to Reclaim Asheville," by Henry Robinson (same paper, issue, and page). North Carolina typically leads the nation in hate crimes against homosexuals.

For a detailed description of "the homosexual lifestyle" in a Nazi concentration camp, see Aras van Hertum, "Survivors of Nazi Camps Begin to Tell Their Stories," *The Washington Blade,* December 3, 1993, p. 1, as well as Heinz Heger's *The Men With the Pink Triangle: The True, Life-and-Death Story of Homosexual Prisoners in the Nazi Concentration Camps,* translation and introduction by David Fernbach (Merlin-Verlag, Hamburg, Germany: 1980), first published as a paperback original by Alyson Publications, Boston (third printing, 1986). (This book, along with the collection at the United States Holocaust Memorial Museum, really makes you wonder how Pat Robertson came to the conclusion that Nazis were in cahoots with gays).

A call to CBN's "prayer line" number "to cure a homosexual friend" resulted in both the CBN *Gay Lib* brochure and a recommendation to call "specialists." Pure Life Ministries was recommended and they graciously sent a number of materials which barely mentioned homosexuality. Steve Gallagher's brochure *The Roots of Sexual Addiction* (Pure Life Ministries, Crittenden, Kentucky, undated) was one of the resulting handful of materials.

The Concise Dictionary of the Christian Condition by J. P. Douglas, Walter A. Elwell, and Peter Toon (Regency Reference Library, an imprint of Zondervan Publishing House, Grand Rapids, MI: 1989) states that ". . . [homosexuality] is primarily a condition, not behavior" (p. 187). Heather Rhoads is quoted from her article "Cruel Crusade: The Holy War Against Lesbians & Gays," *The Progressive,* March 1993, p. 22. FBI 1993 hate-crime statistics quoted from David W. Dunlap, "Survey Details Gay Slayings Around U.S.," *New York Times,* December 21, 1994.

To Provide Spiritual Strength and Acceptance to Homosexuals

For detail on recent scientific findings relating to homosexuality, see Chandler Burr's "Homosexuality and Biology," *The Atlantic Monthly,* March 1993, pp. 47-65; David Gelman, Donna Foote, Todd Barrett, and Mary Talbot, "Born or Bred? Science and Psychiatry Are Struggling to Make Sense of New Research that Suggests that Homosexuality May Be a Matter of Genetics, Not Parenting," *Newsweek,* February 24, 1992, pp. 46-53. For a good explanation of National Institutes of Health data, see Boyce Rensberger, "Study Links Genes to Homosexuality," *The Washington Post,* July 16, 1993, pp. A1, A6; Darrel Yates Rist, "Are Homosexuals Born That Way?" *The Nation,* October 19, 1992 pp. 424-429; and Christopher B. Daly, "Study of Twins Suggests Lesbianism Has a Genetic Component," *The Washington Post,* March 15, 1993, p. A3. The Children of God reference is from a Reuters News Service article in *The Washington Post,* September 2, 1993.

The Mel White quote is from W. Hampton Sides, "The Secret of the Ghostwriter; Mel White Gave Voice to the Christian Right. Then He Committed the Sin of Admission," *The Washington Post,* August 10, 1993, p. B2. The Martin Duberman quote is from Leigh Rutledge, *Unnatural Quotations: A Compendium of Quotations by, for, or About Gay People* (Alyson Publications, Boston: 1988) pp. 22-23. The MCC quote is from Kristina Campbell, "Dallas Dedicates $3 Million Cathedral, *The Washington Blade,* March 12, 1993. Kenneth L. Cuthbertson, Ph.D., is quoted from his article "What the Bible Says About Gays," *The Washington Blade,* November 27, 1992, p. 37.

For information on Gay spiritual issues, see Peg Meier, "Gay Catholics in Exile," Minneapolis *Star/Trib-une,* November 7, 1992, pp. 1E, 10E; Laurie Goldstein, "Ministers Seek Ways to Meet Spiritual Needs of Homosexuals," *The Washington Post,* October 12, 1993, pp. B1, B7; Gustav Spohn, "Denomination for Gays Fails in Bid to Join National Group," *The Washington Post,* November 14, 1992, p. G11; Christopher Herlinger, Religious News Service, "Gays Returning to Religion, But Few Arms Open," *The Washington Post,* June 25, 1994, p. C7; and Russell Cate, "New Catholic Catechism Urges 'Respect' for Gays," *The Washington Blade,* November 27, 1992.

For generally gay-positive reactions from the religious establishment, see Gustav Niebuhr, "Two Bishops Sign Ad Backing Gay Rights," *The Washington Post,* November 1, 1992, p. A4; Matthew Corey, "Lutheran Church Takes a Stand on Gay Unions," *The Washington Blade,* November 5, 1993, p. 28; Robert O'Harrow, Jr., "Gays Welcomed at D.C. Church," *The Washington Post,* June 7, 1993, p. B4; and David E. Anderson, "Sexuality Document 'Biblically Flawed,' " *The Washington Post,* November 27, 1993, p. B7.

On the debate over gay marriage rights, see Eloise Salholz, Lucille Beachy, Dogan Hannan, Vicki Quade, and Melinda Liu, "For Better or Worse," *Newsweek,* May 24, 1993, p. 69.

To Support or Oppose Capital Punishment

For a general background on policies and means of execution, see Paul LaCroix, *Manners, Customs and Dress During the Middle Ages and During the Renaissance Period* (D. Appleton & Company, New York: 1874). Some specific works that provide good perspectives on this subject include Dr. William H. Baker's *On Capital Punishment* (Moody Press, A Ministry of Moody Bible Institute, Chicago: 1985), and his conclusion quoted from p. 156; and *Punishment Human and Divine* by Reverend W. C. de Pauley, B.D. (Society for Promoting Christian Knowledge, London, The MacMillan Company, New York and Toronto: 1925). Also see "Blackmun Reevaluating His Death Penalty Stand," *The Washington Post,* November 19, 1993, p. A4; and Peter Birks and Grant McLeod (introduction and translation) and Paul Krueger (Latin text), *Justinian's Institutes,* Cornell University Press, Ithaca, NY: 1987.

To Mistrust and Persecute Catholics

Excellent surveys of this conflict can be found in Reuben Maury's *The Wars of the Godly* (Robert M. McBride & Company, New York: 1928; Everett R. Clinchy's *All In the Name of God* (The John Day Company, New York: 1934) and Timothy A. Byrnes's *Catholic Bishops in American Politics* (Princeton University Press, Princeton, NJ: 1991). Also see Edwin S. Gaustad's *A Documentary History of Religion in America Since 1865* (William B. Eerdmans Publishing Company, Grand Rapids, MI: 1983; reprinted 1990) for the quotation by John L. Brandt, pp. 262-267. The printed texts of Reverend A. Powell Davies's sermons, including the quotation by George Washington, are "The White House and the Vatican" (October 28, 1951) and "Catholics and American History" (November 11, 1951), as printed by the publications committee of All Souls Church, Unitarian, Washington, D.C. The address of Most Reverend John Ireland, D.D., appears in John A. Ryan, D.D., and Francis J. Boland, C.S.C., Ph.D., *Catholic Principles of Politics* (The MacMillan Company, New York: 1943), p. 348. Also see Mrs. William Lloyd Clark, *Priest and Woman: A Book for Wives, Mothers and Daughters* (no publisher given, Milan, IL: early 1900s, eighth edition).

To Define the Terms of Marriage

Of course, most of the references in the previous chapters that deal with women also deal with marriage. Years of sermons and accumulation of tracts and literature contributed to what even the most literal would call an extremely inflexible definition of the institution. An example of contemporary polygamy is found in the story of El-wood Gallimore in "Polygamy and the Preacher" by Peter Baker, *The Washington Post*, January 27, 1993, pp. D1 and D8. For the Jimmy Carter interview of October, 1976, see *Playboy Collector's Edition 35th Anniversary Issue*, January 1989. The case of *Loving* v. *Virginia* can be reviewed in "Mr. Justice Marshall," *Newsweek*, June 26, 1967, pp. 34-36 and "Anti-Miscegenation Statutes: Repugnant Indeed," *Time*, June 23, 1967, pp. 45-46. For details on the Virginia law, see *Eugenics in Relation to the New Family and the Law on Racial Integrity* (including a paper read before the American Public Health Association), issued by the Bureau of Vital Statistics, State Board of Health, Richmond, Virginia, 1924. The Jimmy Swaggart quote is from "Scandals: No Apologies This Time," *Time Magazine*, October 1991, p. 35. See also Del Martin, *Battered Wives* (Glide Publication, San Francisco: 1976), pp. 29-30.

To Control the Consumption of Alcohol

An excellent feel for the period, the movement's leaders and their arguments, the positions of the churches, and calls for political action can be found in New Hampshire Senator Henry William Blair's *The Temperance Movement: or, The Conflict Between Man and Alcohol* (William E. Smythe Company, Boston: 1887), which includes statements from Mrs. E. F. Thompson. Sample temperance sermons studied included those by Dwight Lyman Moody in *Moody's Gospel & Sermons Delivered in Europe and America* (Rhodes & McClure Publishing Company, Chicago: 1891) and H. M. Wharton in his *Gospel Talks* (R. H. Woodward and Company, Baltimore: 1888), pp. 154-155. The cited temperance hymns are from Asa R. Trowbridge's *The Temperance Melodeon: A Collection of Original Music, Written Expressly for This Work* (Theodore Abbot, Boston: 1844). Also see Roger A. Burns's *Preacher: Billy Sunday & Big-time American Evangelism* (W. W. Norton & Company, New York and London: 1992) and Andrew Sinclair's superb analysis, *Era of Excess: A Social History of the Prohibition Movement*, preface by Richard Hofstadter (Harper Colophon Books, Harper & Row, New York: 1962), from which the Anti-Saloon League's anonymous first lobbyist is quoted.

As Part of a Program of Recovery from Addiction

A good history of the early days of Alcoholics Anonymous is *Dr. Bob and the Good Oldtimers: A Biography, with Recollections of Early A.A. in the Midwest,* by an anonymous author. See p. 54 concerning the Oxford Group ("making a surrender . . ."). (Alcoholics Anonymous World Services, Inc., New York: 1980). Thomas Trotter is quoted in Dr. James R. Milam and Katherine Ketcham's *Under the Influence: A Guide to the Myths and Realities of Alcoholism* (Bantam Books, New York: 1983), p. 136; Also refer to "The Big Book"—*Alcoholics Anonymous: The Story of How Many Thousands of Men and Women Have Recovered from Alcoholism* (Alcoholics Anonymous World Services, Inc.: 1976 and subsequent editions) and other AA literature. Popular works of the day that Dr. Bob read and shared included Henry Drummond's *The Greatest Thing in the World* (Home Book Company, New York, Dresden edition: late nineteenth-century edition); Emmet Fox's *The Sermon on the Mount: The Key to Success in Life and The Lord's Prayer: An Interpretation* (HarperSan-Francisco, A Division of HarperCollins Publishers, 1989 edition; copyright 1932, 1938 by Emmet Fox. Renewed in 1966 by Kathleen Whelan); and William James's *The Varieties of Religious Experience: A Study in Human Nature* (being the Gifford lectures on natural religion delivered at Edinburgh in 1901–1902), forward by Jacque Barzun (Mentor Books, The Penguin Group; reprint).

To Forbid Work and Commerce on Sundays

This history of this subject is covered in detail in David N. Laband and Deborah Hendry Heinbuch's *Blue Laws: The History, Economics, and Politics of Sunday-Closing Laws* (Lexington Books, D. C. Heath and Company, Lexington, MA, and Toronto: 1987). Also see pertinent discussions in Patricia U. Bonomi's *Under the Cope of Heaven: Religion, Society and Politics in Colonial America* (Oxford University Press, New York, Oxford: 1986) and A. James Reichley's *Religion in American Public Life* (The Brookings Institution, Washington, DC: 1985). Also see Reverend W. C. de Pauley, B.D., *Punishment Human and Divine* (Society for Promoting Christian Knowledge, London; New York and Toronto, The MacMillan Company: 1925), pp. 187–188; H. M. Wharton, *Gospel Talks* (R. H. Woodward and Company, Baltimore: 1886), p. 84; and Reverend Dwight Lyman Moody in *Moody's Gospel Sermons* (Rhodes & McClure Publishing Company, Chicago: 1891), p. 159. Huestis is quoted from his *Sunday in the Making* (Abingdon Press, New York: 1929), an extract of which is reprinted in Edwin S. Gaustad's *A Documentary History of Religion in America Since 1865* (William B. Eerdmans Publishing Company, Grand Rapids: 1983, reprinted 1990). For detailed case histories of Sunday baseball, see David T. Javersak's "Wheeling's Sunday Sensation: The 1889 Wheeling Nailers," *Upper Ohio Valley Historical Review 8* (1979, pp. 2–6), source of the Wheeling law and Steven Riess' "Professional Sunday Baseball: A Study in Social Reform, 1892–1934," *Maryland Historian 4* (1973, pp. 95–108).

To Justify or Oppose Prayer in Public Schools

This long-running issue has been extensively discussed in many books dealing with issues of church and state. Among those, see Ann E. Weiss, *God and Government: The Separation of Church and State* (Houghton Mifflin Company, Boston: 1982); Stephen L. Carter, *The Culture of Disbelief: How American Law and Politics Trivialize Religious Devotion* (BasicBooks, a division of HarperCollins Publishers, New York: 1993); Ed. Albert J. Menendez, *The Best of Church & State, 1948–1975* (Americans United for Separation of Church and State, Silver Spring, Maryland: 1975); and A. James Reichley, *Religion in American Public Life* (The Brookings Institution, Washington, DC: 1985). The story of Dr. Bishop Knox received wide media coverage from December 1993 through February 1994 and sporadically thereafter; see Vern & Smith, "A Principal's

Troubling Prayer," *Newsweek,* December 20, 1993, p. 107; also see William Booth, "Bring Back School Prayer? That's Rallying Cry in Mississippi," *The Washington Post,* December 20, 1993, p. A1. The information on Vista, California, schools is from an ACLU fundraising letter, 1994. Jerry Falwell is quoted from his book *America Can Be Saved* (1979), as excerpted in *The Religious Right...* page 6; Also obtained from Alan M. Schwartz, editor, *The Religious Right* (Anti-Defamation League, New York: 1994) the Lou Sheldon quote (p. 4) and the Simonds information (p. 101). For an overview of prayer in America, including poll results on the frequency of prayer, see "Talking to God" by Kenneth L. Woodward et al., *Newsweek,* January 6, 1992, pp. 38–44. Bill Clinton quote: John F. Harris, "Clinton Says Schools Can't Bar Religion," *The Washington Post,* July 13, 1995, pp. A1, A6.

To Oppose or Embrace Medical Science

The history and beliefs of Christian Science were reviewed in John DeWitt's *The Christian Science Way of Life* (The Christian Science Publishing Society, Boston: 1962) and Charles Francis Potter's *The Story of Religion Told in the Lives of Its Leaders* (Garden City Publishing Company, Inc., Garden City, NY: 1929). Also refer to Mary Baker Eddy, *Science and Health with Key to the Scriptures* (First Church of Christ, Scientist, Boston: 1971). The Gittens quote appeared in *The Washington Post,* "Parents Cleared in Son's Death," an Associated Press article, August 12, 1993, p. A7. The Ronald Cole-Turner quote is from Christine Lehmann, "Gene Research Poses New Ethical Dilemmas," *The Washington Post,* December 18, 1993, p. B7. Quotes from Kevorkian trial and videotape are from Associated Press article, "Kevorkian Tape Shows Man's Plea to Die," *The Washington Post,* August 28, 1993, p. A5. Also from *The Washington Post,* see the news service story on Reverend Ted Peters (August 20, 1994, p. D9); "Gene Research Poses New Ethical Dilemmas," Christine Lehmann (December 18, 1993, p. B6); an Associated Press story,

"Wrongful Death Findings May Mean More Damages in Christian Science Case" (August 21, 1993, p. A10); and "State Can't Force Woman to Have Cesarean Section, Illinois Appeals Panel Says," Edward Walsh (December 15, 1993, p. A3).

To Oppose or Justify War

Sources reviewed and recommended for their in-depth discussions include John Driver's *How Christians Made Peace with War: Early Christian Understandings of War* (Peace and Justice Series 2, Herald Press, Scottdale, PA and Kitchener, Ontario: 1988); Ralph Luther Moellering's *Modern War and the Christian* (Augsburg Publishing House, Minneapolis, MN: 1969); J. Carter Swaim's *War, Peace and the Bible* (Orbis Books, Maryknoll, NY: 1982); and Roland H. Bainton's *Christian Attitudes Toward War and Peace: A Historical Survey and Critical Re-evaluation* (Abingdon Press: New York, Nashville: 1960). "The Four B's" from Laurie Goodstein's " 'Agents of God' Practice a Christianity Few Would Recognize," *The Washington Post,* May 20, 1995, p. A12. The quotations concerning the Pearl Harbor Day, 1993, incident in North Carolina are from a feature on National Public Radio's *All Things Considered,* Saturday, August 20, 1994. See Edwin Greenlaw and James Holly Hanford, editors, *The Great Tradition* (Scott, Foresman and Company, Chicago, IL and New York: 1919) for the Lincoln quotation from his second inaugural address (p. 576), and Kaiser Wilhelm II as quoted in an address by David Lloyd George in "The Case Against Germany" on September 19, 1914 (p. 606). Thomas Paine is quoted from *The American Crisis,* Number 5, March 21, 1778. The lyrics to "Onward Christian Soldiers" were written by Reverend Sabine Baring-Gould in 1864 and published in *Musical Times* (London: 1877), p. 311. Pat Buchanan's "Cultural War" statements from Alan M. Schwartz, editor, *The Religious Right* (Anti-Defamation League, New York: 1994) p. 40.

To Prove That the Earth Is the Center of the Universe

James J. Walsh's *The Popes and Science: The History of the Papal Relations to Science During the Middle Ages and Down to Our Own Time* (Knights of Columbus Edition, Fordham University Press, New York: 1911) argues that Galileo was the exception rather than the rule in any church-sponsored campaigns against scientific inquiry (quotation from p. 17). There are many biographies and historical analyses dealing with Galileo, his life, and times. For an overview, see Jack Meadows's *The Great Scientists: The Story of Science Told Through the Lives of Twelve Landmark Figures* (Oxford University Press, New York: 1987); and Giorgio de Santillana, *The Crime of Galileo* (Time Incorporated, New York: 1962). Also see Nancy Hathaway's *The Friendly Guide to the Universe* (Viking, published by the Penguin Group, New York: 1994) and Stillman Drake's *Discoveries and Opinions of Galileo* (Anchor Books, New York: 1957) as well as his *Galileo* (Oxford University Press: New York, 1980); "Letter to Christina" is quoted from *Galileo,* p. 6. James J. Walsh is quoted from his book *The Popes and Science* (Fordham University Press, New York: 1911), p. 17.

To Prove That God Created Man and the Universe

To review the drama in Dayton, Tennessee, see Mary Lee Settle's *The Scopes Trial: The State of Tennessee v. John Thomas Scopes* (Franklin Watts, Inc., New York: 1972) and Tom McGowen's *The Great Monkey Trial: Science vs. Fundamentalism in America* (Franklin Watts, A Twentieth Century American History Book, New York, London, Toronto, Sydney: 1990). Also see the excellent account and discussion of this and other relevant issues in Garry Wills, *Under God: Religion and American Politics* (Simon and Schuster, New York: 1990). Falwell is quoted from Phil Donahue, *The Human Animal* (Simon and Schuster, New York: 1985), p.

38. Reverend Chambers is quoted from Jennifer Bush, "Names & Faces," *The Washington Post,* November 27, 1993, p. F3. Also see Gerald L. Schroeder, Ph.D., *Genesis and the Big Bang: The Discovery of Harmony Between Modern Science and the Bible* (Bantam Books, New York: 1992), p. 29; see p. 163 for the quotation from Pope Pius XII. General references include Conrad Hyers' *The Meaning of Creation: Genesis and Modern Science* (John Knox Press, Atlanta: 1984); Ronald L. Numbers' *The Creationists: The Evolution of Scientific Creationism* (Alfred A. Knopf: 1992); Peter Zetterberg, editor, *Evolution and Public Education* (University of Minnesota, St. Paul: 1981); and by James W. Skehan, S.J., Ph.D., *Modern Science and the Book of Genesis* (Science Compacts from the National Science Teachers Association: 1986).

To Exploit or Save the Environment

In recent years, many sermons, Sunday School classes, books, newsletters and mailings, and articles in newspapers and magazines have focused on this issue. Examples include "Eco-Myths: Don't believe everything you hear about the Church and the environmental crisis" in *Christianity Today* (April 4, 1994); essays by David N. Livingstone, Calvin B. DeWitt, Loren Wilkinson, and Kenneth S. Kantzer; and *Earth & Spirit: The Spiritual Dimension of the Environmental Crisis,* edited by Fritz Hull (Continuum Publishing Company, New York: 1993), which includes Miriam Therese MacGillis's essay "Food as Sacrament." One of the comprehensive resource guides for Earth Day 1994 observances in churches is by Shantilal P. Bhagat, editor, *God's Earth—Our Home: A Resource for Congregational Study and Action on Environmental and Economic Justice* (National Council of Churches of Christ in the USA, New York, 1994). For an example of media coverage, see "Religions Take 'Earth Day' Leap Into Environmental Theology," Michael J. Paquette, *The Washington Post,* April 16, 1994, p. B7. Also see the National Staff of Environmental Action (editors), *Earth Day—The Begin-*

ning: A Guide for Survival (Bantam Books, New York: 1970); Reverend Phillips' quotation from p. 73. Sister Miriam Therese MacGillis is quoted from an article by Colman McCarthy, "In N.J., Nuns Cultivate a Spiritual-Ecological Link on Genesis Farm," *The Washington Post,* October 2, 1993, pp. B6–7.

To Predict the Time of the End of the World

A good early overview of coming events, apocalyptic terms, and prophetic figures is by a disciple of William Miller, Joshua V. Himes, in *The Bible Student's Manual of Chronology and Prophecy, Selected from the Works of William Miller; with a Chronological Chart, Recently Prepared by Him* (Moses A. Dow, Boston: 1841). On Miller, also see Clara Endicott Sears's *Days of Delusion: A Strange Bit of History* (Houghton Mifflin Company, New York: 1924) and *The Midnight Cry: A Defense of William Miller and the Millerites* by Francis D. Nichol (Ministerial Association of Seventh-Day Adventists, Review and Herald Publishing, Washington, D.C.: 1944). Also, see Ellen Gould White's *The Great Controversy,* which has appeared in various editions over the last century (e.g., for Remnant Publications, Inc., Pacific Press Publishing Association, Boise ID: 1992). Two exceptional books dealing with this subject are Paul Boyer's *When Time Shall Be No More: Prophecy Belief in Modern American Culture* (Harvard University Press: 1992) and Garry Wills's *Under God: Religion and American Politics* (Simon and Schuster, New York: 1990). Armstrong's explanation from *Plain Truth?* of November 1971 is quoted by James Morris in *The Preachers* (St. Martin's Press, New York: 1973). Also see "A Brief History of the End of Time," Cate Plys, *Washington City Paper,* June 24, 1994, pp. 17–20. Ronald Reagan is quoted from Alan M. Schwartz, editor, *The Religious Right* (Anti-Defamation League, New York: 1994), p. 152. Also see Hal Lindsey (with C. C. Carlson), *The Late Great Planet Earth* (Zondervan, Grand Rapids: 1970).

Further Reading

In addition to the many books and articles listed in the Notes section, the reader is directed to the following selection of superb general resources, which cover a wide range of issues:

Paul J. Achtemeier, editor, *Harper's Bible Dictionary* (The Society of Biblical Literature, Harper San Francisco: 1985).

Harold Bloom, *The American Religion: The Emergence of the Post-Christian Nation* (Simon & Schuster, New York: 1992).

Stephen L. Carter, *The Culture of Disbelief: How American Law and Politics Trivialize Religious Devotion* (BasicBooks, a division of HarperCollins, New York: 1993).

Everett R. Clinchy, *All in the Name of God* (The John Day Company, New York: 1934).

Cain Hope Felder, *Troubling Biblical Waters: Race, Class, and Family* (Orbis Books, Maryknoll, New York: 1989).

Edwin S. Gaustad, *A Documentary History of Religion in America Since 1865* (William B. Eerdmans Publishing Company, Grand Rapids, MI: 1983, reprinted 1990).

Edwin Greenlaw, editor, *The Great Tradition: A Book of Selections from English and American Prose and Poetry, Illustrating the National Ideals of Freedom, Faith, and Conduct* (Scott, Foresman and Company, New York: 1919).

The Holy Bible (Robinson, Pratt Co., New York: 1842).

Paul LaCroix, *Manners, Customs and Dress During the Middle Ages and During the Renaissance Period* (D. Appleton & Company, New York: 1874).

Vincent L. Milner, *Religious Denominations of the World* (Bradley, Garretson & Co., Philadelphia: 1873).

Charles Francis Potter, *The Story of Religion Told in the Lives of Its Leaders* (Garden City Publishing Company, Inc., Garden City, NY: 1929).

Uta Ranke-Heinemann, *Eunuchs for the Kingdom of Heaven: Women, Sexuality and the Catholic Church*, translated by Peter Heinegg (New York: Penguin Books, 1991; reprinted by arrangement with Doubleday).

John Romer, *Testament: The Bible and History* (Henry Holt and Company, New York: 1988).

Alan M. Schwartz, editor, *The Religious Right: The Assault on Tolerance & Pluralism in America* (Anti-Defamation League, New York: 1994).

John Shelby Spong, *Rescuing the Bible from Fundamentalism: A Bishop Rethinks the Meaning of Scripture* (HarperSanFrancisco: 1992).

Reverend Nathaniel West, D.D., *The Complete Analysis of the Holy Bible* (A. J. Johnson, New York: 1869).

Photo/Illustration Sources

p. ii   "This is the Enemy," U.S. World War II propaganda poster, c. 1938. Courtesy National Archive, Washington, DC.

p. 3   Harper's Weekly, October 15, 1864, pp. 664–665. Detail from "The Chicago Platform" by Thomas Nast. Authors' collection.

p. 4   Benezet, Anthony. "Observations on the Inslaving, importing and purchasing of Negroes; . . . extracted from . . . the Yearly-Meeting of Quakers," 1760. Title page. Library of Congress, Washington, DC. (LC-USZ62-57335).

p. 5   "Flogging the Negro," woodcut by M. Vaningen-Snyder, 1864.

p. 6   "The History of the Old/New Testament; being an historical account . . . Illustrated with Sculptures . . . Translated from the Works of the Learned Le Sieur De Royaumont, London. Printed in the Year MDCCIII." (PLATE 30)

p. 7   "Pictorial Illustration of Abolitionism . . . Its Rise, Progress and End." Undated. Broadside collection, portfolio 100–46. Lot 4422A, Library of Congress, Washington, DC. (LC-USZ62-40831).

p. 8   "The Liberty Bell" (Anti-Slavery Society, Boston: 1839). Authors' collection.

p. 9   TOP Illustration from Uncle Tom's Cabin by Harriet Beecher Stowe. Undated. Classified as "Illustrations: 1880–1930." Library of Congress, Washington, DC. (LC-USZC4-2573).

p. 9   BOTTOM Detail of broadside by John Greenley, New York: 1837. Woodcut. Rare Book Collection, Library of Congress, Washington, DC. Portfolio 118, #32A. (LC-USZ62-44265).

p. 10   Center for Democratic Renewal, Atlanta, GA, 1992.

p. 11   Library of Congress, Washington, DC. Circa 1920.

p. 12   Detail of sheet music art for "Hurrah for the Ku Klux Klan 1920s" Library of Congress, Washington, DC.

p. 13   Illustration by Rand Cheadle, 1994.

p. 14   Illustration by Rand Cheadle, 1994.

p. 15   Scribner's Monthly, conducted by J. G. Holland (Scribner & Company: 1875).

p. 16   TOP "The History of the Old/New Testament; being an historical account . . . Illustrated with Sculptures . . . Translated from the Works of the Learned Le Sieur De Royaumont, London. Printed in the Year MDCCIII." (Plate 160)

p. 16   BOTTOM "The History of the Old/New Testament; being an historical account . . . Illustrated with Sculptures . . . Translated from the Works of the Learned Le Sieur De Royaumont, London. Printed in the Year MDCCIII." (Plate 217)

p. 17   Photograph by Thomas O'Halloran, September 22, 1963. US News & World Report Collection, Library of Congress, Washington, DC. Frame #6A. (LC-U9-10515)

p. 18   Photograph by Marion S. Trikosko, March 26, 1964. US News and World Report Collection, Library of Congress, Washington, DC. Frame #9A. (LC-U9-11696)

p. 19   Photograph by Rand Cheadle. 1994.

p. 20   Arnold Kramer, United States Holocaust Memorial Museum, Washington, DC. Circa 1940.

p. 21   TOP LaCroix, Paul. "Manners, Customs and Dress During the Middle Ages, and During the Renaissance Period." (D. Appleton and Company, New

York: 1874, p. 444). Woodcut in the "Liber Chroni-carum Mundi": large folio, Nuremberg, 1493.

p. 21   BOTTOM "The History of the Old/New Testament; being an historical account . . . Illustrated with Sculptures . . . Translated from the Works of the Learned Le Sieur De Royaumont, London. Printed in the Year MDCCIII." (Plate 206)

p. 22   LaCroix, Paul. "Manners, Customs and Dress During the Middle Ages, and During the Renaissance Period." (D. Appleton and Company, New York: 1874; p. 452). Facsimile of woodcut in Boaistuau's "Histoires Prodigieuses," Paris, Annet Briere, 1560. (Nineteenth-century facsimile of a woodcut of 1560.)

p. 23   From a photograph of the Reverend Fr. Charles E. Coughlin, 1933. Photographer unknown. Library of Congress, Washington, DC. (LC-USZ62-38494)

p. 24   National Library of Medicine woodcut of 1493 by Hartmann Schelel (1410–1485) from Schedel, "Liber chronicarum Nuremberg," Anton Koberger, July 12, 1493.

p. 25   Photo of daguerreotype of Elizabeth Cady Stanton with daughter Harriot, 1856. Library of Congress, Washington, DC. (LC-USZ62-48965)

p. 27   E. W. Gustin, 1909. Library of Congress, Washington, DC. (LC-USZ62-51821)

p. 28   Anonymous photograph dated 1891. Authors' collection.

p. 29   "Interior of the Cathedral at Bourges" by Pierre Gaston Rigaud (1920). Oil on panel. Collection of Rand Cheadle.

p. 30   TOP Corel Corporation.

p. 30   BOTTOM Authors' illustration/photograph.

p. 31   *Cassell's Doré Gallery,* introduction by Edmund Ollier. (Cassell & Company, Limited, London, Paris and New York: 1885.) Authors' collection. (Plate 100)

p. 34   National Library of Medicine illustration in Petrarca, Francesco "Von der artzney bayder Gluck, des guten und wilderwetigen," Augsburg, Heynrich Steyner, 1532 B. 1, 1.9 verso.

p. 35   Authors' photograph in Rare Book Division, Library of Congress, Washington, DC.

p. 36   Rare Book Division, Library of Congress, Washington, DC. Author's photograph.

p. 36   Rare Book Division, Library of Congress, Washington, DC. Authors' photograph.

p. 37   *Cassell's Doré Gallery,* introduction by Edmund Ollier. (Cassell & Company, Limited, London, Paris and New York: 1885.) Authors' collection. (Plate 230)

p. 38   The Quaker Collection, Haverford College Library.

p. 39   TOP *Philadelphia: Quakerkirche,* In Ernest von Hess-Wartburg, Nord Amerika, 1888. Library of Congress, Washington, DC. (LC-USZ62-2511)

p. 39   BOTTOM The Quaker Collection, Haverford College Library.

p. 40   Corel Corporation.

p. 42   "Why Should Priests Wed?" by "J.C." (A. E. Costello, New York: 1888.) Authors' collection.

p. 44   "The History of the Old/New Testament; being an historical account . . . Illustrated with Sculptures . . . Translated from the Works of the Learned Le Sieur De Royaumont, London. Printed in the Year MDCCIII." (Plate 17)

Photo/Ilustration Sources

p. 68   United States Holocaust Memorial Museum, Washington, DC.

p. 70   LaCroix, Paul. "Manners, Customs and Dress During the Middle Ages, and During the Renaissance Period." (D. Appleton and Company, New York: 1874; p. 415). Facsimile of woodcut of the "Cosmographie Universelle" of Munster: in folio, Basle, 1552. From a nineteenth-century facsimile of a woodcut of 1552.

p. 71   *A Brief History of Ancient, Mediaeval, and Modern Peoples, With Some Account of their Monuments, Institutions, Arts, Manners and Customs* (A.S. Barnes & Co., New York & Chicago: pre-1900, undated).

p. 72   Illustration in T. Dewitt Talmadge, D.D., *Social Dynamite, or the Wickedness of Modern Society* (Standard Publishing, Chicago: 1890; p. 257).

p. 73   Shocking Gray. (800) 788-4729.

p. 75   Photo by Rand Cheadle, 1993.

p. 76   *Cassell's Doré Gallery,* introduction by Edmund Ollier (Cassell & Company, Limited, London, Paris and New York: 1885). Authors' collection. (Plate 84)

p. 77   Photo. co. by Hamilton's Drug Store, 1908. Library of Congress, Washington, DC.

p. 78   The Complete Woodcuts of Albrecht Dürer (Dover Publications, New York: 1963).

p. 79   "Adjusting the Noose," February 12, 1906. Library of Congress, Washington, DC. (LC-USZ62-26374)

p. 81   LaCroix, Paul. "Manners, Customs and Dress During the Middle Ages, and During the Renaissance Period." (D. Appleton and Company, New York: 1874). Bibl. imp. de Paris.

p. 82   Corel Corporation.

p. 83   Wood engraving from "Balleu's Pictorial Drawing-Room Companion," 1855. Library of Congress, Washington, DC. (LC-USZ62-2752)

p. 84   Engravings from *New England Primer* by D. L. Ford. Library of Congress, Washington, DC. (LC-USZ62-51683)

p. 88   Illustration in *Social Dynamite, or The Wickedness of Modern Society,* T. DeWitt Talmadge, D.D. (Standard Publishing, Chicago: 1890; p. 117). Authors' collection.

p. 90   Booklet printed in 1924 by Bureau of Vital Statistics, State Board of Health, Richmond, VA. Authors' collection.

p. 91   Title page of *What Miscegenation Is!* L. Seaman, LL.D. (Waller & Willetts, Publishers, New York: 1864). Library of Congress, Washington, DC. (LC-USZ62-32501)

p. 92   Photograph from *The Temperance Movement, or the Conflict Between Man and Alcohol,* Henry William Blair (William E. Smythe Company, Boston: 1888; p. 511).

p. 93   Wood engraving by Thomas Nast in *Harper's Weekly,* June 13, 1874. Library of Congress, Washington, DC. (LC-USZ62-36252)

p. 94   Photo taken April 27, 1915. (Underwood & Underwood.) Library of Congress, Washington, DC. (LC-USZ62-7473)

p. 94   LEFT "The History of the Old/New Testament; being an historical account . . . Illustrated with Sculptures . . . Translated from the Works of the Learned Le Sieur De Royaumont, London. Printed in the Year MDCCIII." (Plate 166)

p. 95   *The Dry Years: Selected Photographs on Prohibition from the Collections of the Library of Congress* (Photo by National Photo Co., 1923). Library of Congress, Washington, DC. (LC-USZ62-15182)

p. 96   Photo by Rand Cheadle, 1971.

p. 98   Seymour, Robert (1800?–1836), artist. "Night-Morning" etched by Shortshanks, 26 Haymarket St., London, England. National Library of Medicine, Bethesda, MD.

p. 99   W. A. Rogers cartoon from the New York *Herald,* March 15, 1908. Library of Congress, Washington, DC. (LC-USZ62-17327)

p. 100   *Cassell's Doré Gallery,* introduction by Edmund Ollier (Cassell & Company, Limited, London, Paris and New York: 1885). Authors' collection. (Plate 59)

p. 101   Photo by Rand Cheadle, 1994.

p. 102   Mitchell, Donald G. *American Lands and Letters* (Scribners, New York: 1897; p. 9).

p. 103   Authors' collection.

p. 104   "The public-school question,—What sectarian appropriation of the school fund is doing. And what it may lead to." Drawing by Bellew for *Harper's Weekly,* August 30, 1873. Library of Congress, Washington, DC. (LC-USZ62-2018)

p. 105   KKK sheet music cover, Library of Congress, Washington, DC.

p. 108   "The History of the Old/New Testament; being an historical account . . . Illustrated with Sculptures . . . Translated from the Works of the Learned Le Sieur De Royaumont, London. Printed in the Year MDCCIII." (Plate 186)

p. 109   "Clerici Regulares," not dated. Prints and Photographs Collection, National Library of Medicine, Bethesda, MD.

p. 110   Library of Congress, Washington, DC.

p. 111   *Cassell's Doré Gallery,* introduction by Edmund Ollier (Cassell & Company, Limited, London, Paris and New York: 1885). Authors' collection. (Plate 148)

p. 112   Prints and Photographs Collection, National Library of Medicine, Bethesda, MD.

p. 113   Authors' photograph.

p. 114   Crusades image from a school textbook in the Barnes General History Series, *A Brief History of Ancient, Medieval, and Modern Peoples* (A. S. Barnes & Co., New York: c. 1890).

p. 115   Haverford College Library.

p. 116   "The History of the Old/New Testament; being an historical account . . . Illustrated with Sculptures . . . Translated from the Works of the Learned Le Sieur De Royaumont, London. Printed in the Year MDCCIII."

p. 117   Facsimile of Albrecht Dürer woodcut from *Scribner's Magazine,* Vol. XIX, 1879.

p. 118   LEFT "The History of the Old/New Testament; being an historical account . . . Illustrated with Sculptures . . . Translated from the Works of the Learned Le Sieur De Royaumont, London. Printed in the Year MDCCIII."

p. 118   LEFT Gift of the Old Print Shop, 11-7-62. Library of Congress, Washington, DC. (LC-USZ62-23912)

p. 119   LEFT *The Complete Woodcuts of Albrecht Dürer* (Dover Publications, New York: 1963). (Plate 295)

p. 119   RIGHT *Social Dynamite: or, The Wickedness of Modern Society,* T. DeWitt Talmadge, D.D. (Standard Publishing Company, Chicago: 1890).

p. 120   *Milton's Poetical Works,* edited by Sir Egerton Brydges, illustrated with engravings, designed by John Martin and J. W. M. Turner, R. A. Crosby; engraved by Glover. (Nichols, Lee & Company, Boston: 1860; pp. 280–281.) Authors' collection.

p. 122   Frontispiece from *Le Monde avant la Creation de l'Homme* (Schulz et Thullie, Paris: 1857). Authors' collection.

p. 124   Oregon State Board of Health, National Library of Medicine, Bethesda, MD.

p. 125   Authors' collection.

p. 126   Mitchell, S. Augustus. *Mitchell's School Geography/A System of Modern Geography . . .* (Thomas, Cowperthwait & Co., Philadelphia: 1847; p. 158).

p. 127   TOP Photograph by Jack Delano, U.S. Department of Agriculture/Farm Security Administration. Library of Congress, Washington, DC. (LC-USF-33-20960-M4)

p. 127   BOTTOM "The History of the Old/New Testament; being an historical account . . . Illustrated with Sculptures . . . Translated from the Works of the Learned Le Sieur De Royaumont, London. Printed in the Year MDCCIII." (Plate 200)

p. 128   CENTER *American Lands and Letters,* Donald G. Mitchell (Scribner & Sons, New York: 1897; p. 43). Authors' collection.

p. 128   LEFT Photograph by Marion Post Wolcott, 1940. U.S. Department of Agriculture/Farm Security Administration. Library of Congress, Washington, DC. (LC-USF 34-56459-D)

p. 129   "The History of the Old/New Testament; being an historical account . . . Illustrated with Sculptures . . . Translated from the Works of the Learned Le Sieur De Royaumont, London. Printed in the Year MDCCIII." (Plate 230)

p. 130   *The Complete Woodcuts of Albrecht Dürer* (Dover Publications, New York: 1963). (Plate 295)

About the Authors

RAND CHEADLE was born and raised in the Applachian South, growing up in a close Missouri Synod Lutheran Family. He at one time considered a career in theology before deciding on the communications field. He is currently a freelance writer in Washington, D.C.

JIM HILL, a native of Atlanta, Georgia, was raised in a loving Southern Baptist family. A freelance art director, designer, and writer, he also resides in the Washington area.